25.3.07.

for Ian and Harriet
warm regards
from
Denis,

THE INTERNAL
AND EXTERNAL WORLDS
OF CHILDREN
AND ADOLESCENTS

THE CASSEL HOSPITAL MONOGRAPH SERIES

THE CASSEL HOSPITAL MONOGRAPH SERIES

THE INTERNAL AND EXTERNAL WORLDS OF CHILDREN AND ADOLESCENTS

Collaborative Therapeutic Care

Edited by

Lesley Day and Denis Flynn

Paul Coombe	*Lesley Day*
Deirdre Dowling	*Denis Flynn*
Kevin Healy	*Lee Marsden*
Lisa Morice	*Steve McCluskey*
Joanne Turner	

KARNAC

LONDON   NEW YORK

First published in 2003 by
H. Karnac (Books) Ltd.
6 Pembroke Buildings, London NW10 6RE

British Library Cataloguing in Publication Data

A C.I.P. for this book is available from the British Library

ISBN: 1-85575-928-4

10 9 8 7 6 5 4 3 2 1

Edited, designed, and produced by Communication Crafts

Printed in Great Britain

www.karnacbooks.com

CONTENTS

v

ACKNOWLEDGEMENTS

The following have been adapted and reproduced by permission:

Chapter two, from Paul Coombe, "The Inpatient Psychotherapy of a Mother and Child at the Cassel Hospital: A Case of Munchhausen Syndrome by Proxy", *British Journal of Psychotherapy*, 12 (1995).

Chapter three, from Deirdre Dowling, "Poison Glue: The Child's Experience of Munchhausen Syndrome by Proxy", *Journal of Child Psychotherapy*, 24 (2, 1998). (http://www.tandf.co.uk)

Chapter four, from Denis Flynn, "Psychoanalytic Aspects of Inpatient Treatment of Abused Children", *Journal of Child Psychotherapy*, 24 (2, 1998). (http://www.tandf.co.uk)

Extract from Dante's *The Divine Comedy* (Inferno, Canto XVI, 124), translated by Charles H. Sisson (Oxford: Oxford University Press, 1993), reproduced by permission.

* * *

Editors' note: Throughout, all clinical material has been appropriately disguised to protect confidentiality.

CONTRIBUTORS

Paul Coombe worked at the Cassel Hospital as Commonwealth Senior Registrar for three years, on the Families Service, and as manager of the Children's Centre. He trained in adult psychiatry, child psychiatry, and adult psychotherapy in Melbourne, Australia. He is a member of the Australian Association of Group Psychotherapists and an associate member of the Group Analytic Society (London). Currently, he works as a psychoanalytic psychotherapist in private practice in Melbourne. His publications include papers on the individual psychotherapy of eating disorders, the psychodynamics of small and large groups, and family therapy.

Lesley Day, BA, MSc (Econ), MSc (Psychotherapy), Dip. Integ. Psychotherapy, is Head of Cassel Services at the Cassel Hospital and an Adult Psychotherapist in private practice. She undertook her adult psychotherapy training at Metanoia Institute. Prior to joining the Cassel in 1996, she was a Senior Lecturer in Social Science at Brunel University and a policy adviser in the field of child and family social services. She has published in the fields of policy, social work, and psychotherapy.

Deirdre Dowling trained at the British Association of Psychotherapy and is the Head Child Psychotherapist on the Families Service at the Cassel Hospital. Previously she worked as a social worker, manager, and trainer in child care. She has a particular interest in parent/infant work, working with severely deprived families, and teaching and consulting other professionals interested in applying psychoanalytic ideas to their work with families.

Denis Flynn is Consultant Adolescent Psychotherapist and Head of the In-patient Adolescent Unit at the Cassel Hospital and works in private psychoanalytic practice. Previously he worked as a Child Psychotherapist, then Head Child Psychotherapist on the Families Service. He studied philosophy and then worked as a probation officer and social worker, before training as a child psychotherapist at the Tavistock Clinic and as a psychoanalyst with the British Psychoanalytical Society. He is a Member of the British Psychoanalytical Society and works also in private practice as a psychoanalyst. His papers on work with children and adolescents are to be published in a book entitled *The Vital Response*.

Kevin Healy is from Dublin and trained in psychiatry there. He is a Consultant Psychotherapist and has been Clinical Director of the Cassel Hospital since 1997. Initially, he developed an adult inpatient service at the Cassel and then set up the Adolescent Inpatient Service for 16- to 20-year-olds in 1994, where he was the Consultant for three years. He has a particular interest in user empowerment and evidence-based clinical practice within a therapeutic community.

Lee Marsden, BA, PGCE, Dip Educational Therapy, first taught in London comprehensive schools and then at Simmons House Adolescent Unit in North London. After several years as a teacher in the Day Unit of the Tavistock Clinic, she moved to the Cassel Children's Centre. She trained as an educational therapist at Regent's College, London, and contributes to the educational therapy training now based at Caspari House in Islington. She is an active member of the Caspari Foundation and co-editor of their journal, *Educational Therapy and Therapeutic Teaching*.

Lisa Morice trained at the Tavistock Clinic, has been Senior Adolescent Psychotherapist on the Cassel Adolescent Inpatient Unit for the last eight years, and has extensive experience of the treatment of adolescent disturbance. She has also worked as a psychotherapist at Imperial College, London, and as a senior psychiatric social worker in Child Guidance in London. She is a graduate of English Literature from Washington, DC, and following her Masters in Social Work she practised as a psychiatric social worker in the United States before coming to England.

Steve McCluskey, RMN, Cassel Cert, MA (Psychoanalytic Observational Studies), worked as a psychosocial nurse at the Cassel Hospital from 1992 to 1997. Currently, he is working as Deputy Clinical Nurse Manager at the Henderson Hospital, after taking up senior nursing posts in Perinatal Psychiatry and at the Crisis Recovery Unit at the Bethlem Royal Hospital.

Joanne Turner, RMN, Cassel Cert., is a senior nurse at the Cassel Hospital, where she has worked for ten years. She has practised psychosocial nursing on the Adolescent and Families Services and currently works as the outreach nurse on the Adult Service. Previously she worked at the Maudsley Hospital in the forensic service.

CHAPTER ONE

Introduction: public and private dimensions of therapeutic work with children and adolescents

Lesley Day

This monograph brings together a collection of papers about inpatient therapeutic work with children, adolescents, and their families at the Cassel Hospital. The Cassel is one of a small number of national specialist services for people with a severe personality disorder. The treatment offered is psychosocial nursing and psychoanalytic psychotherapy within the therapeutic milieu of the inpatient hospital community.

The intensive and specialist nature of the assessment and treatment that is undertaken with these multi-problem families is described in a detailed exploration of the clinical work with children and their parents in the Families Service. Very often the situation involves a child who has been living in an abusive family; the work is about reaching a decision on the best interests of the child and assessing and working with the potential for parents to care for their child and provide a safe environment. In the Adolescent Service, young people aged 16 to 20 years come to the Cassel for intensive residential psychotherapeutic treatment. This is a Tier-4 service for adolescents with severe disturbance who have often previously accessed other child and adolescent mental health services.

What binds these children, adolescents, and families together, despite their different biographies and mental health problems, is that the Cassel may be a psychotherapeutic place of "last resort" for referrers and patients. As this Monograph documents, the Cassel offers a very different kind of treatment from that provided by "traditional" psychiatry. The stakes are high, and this can create anxiety and ambivalence about the work in staff and feelings of anger, hope, and hopelessness in the patients. The chapters in this Monograph give testimony to these feelings and also explore how they can be worked with and contained in the hospital community structures.

What we also know is that we are working in a child and adolescent mental health service that is itself relatively young and has a chequered history. Notions of childhood and adolescence are relatively modern concepts in Western societies (Aries, 1985; Kroger, 1996), and it is only with the prolonged economic dependence of what we now term "adolescence" that social scientists and clinicians became interested in the emotional and social lives of young people. Psychodynamic theories of adolescence have developed alongside these societal changes (Anderson & Dartington, 1998; Flynn, 2000). Separate mental health services for adolescents were not established until the late 1940s, and Children's Departments came into being after the Second World War dedicated to provide preventative and caring services for children deprived of a "normal home life" (Parton, 1991). Subsequent government reports, audits, and research have, however, documented that there is a wide variation in mental health services provided for children and young people and that the expenditure and provision of services does not correspond to need (Audit Commission, 1999). It appears that despite developments in provision, child and adolescent mental health services remain a Cinderella service. The Audit Commission (1999) found that health authority spending on child and adolescent mental health services accounted, on average, for about 5% of the total amount of spending on mental health services.

This needs to be set against the fact that recent epidemiological studies suggest a prevalence rate of diagnosable disorder of 20% in children and adolescents in the United Kingdom and that

approximately 10–15% of these will be offered treatment by specialist mental health professionals (Audit Commission, 1999; Target & Fonagy, 1996). The Audit Commission found that over
one-third of the trusts they audited reported that they could "not
respond effectively to young people presenting in crisis" (1999, p.
47) and that often the clinical staffing of services was the result of
"historical service patterns" rather than an assessment of need.
Furthermore, the absence of specialized treatment programmes
for post-16-year-old adolescents continues to result in the inappropriate placement of older adolescents in adult mental health services (Audit Commission, 1999).

The paucity of mental health services means that many children, adolescents, and their families do not receive the psychotherapeutic treatment that they need. The consequence of this may
be mental illness in adulthood and generational cycles of psychological disturbance and abuse. If ignored, these social and psychological problems do not simply go away. Indeed, they are likely to
increase the demands on adult mental health services. Target and
Fonagy (1996), for example, point out that children who have
symptoms of depression and anxiety are referred less frequently
to mental health services than those who are diagnosed as having
disruptive disorders. Yet we know that children and adolescents
with symptoms of depression are three times more likely, as
adults, to make a suicide attempt or be hospitalized than matched
non-depressed children in the mental health system (Target &
Fonagy, 1996).

This suggests that what is seen as disturbing about children
and adolescents' mental health may be focused more on their
behaviour and conduct than on their emotional and inner worlds.
Children and adolescents are dependent on parents—and on other
adults with whom they come into regular contact—to be aware of
their psychological needs and difficulties, but it may be the care-
givers' needs rather than the child's that is the spur to seeking
help. If the parents themselves have mental health problems,
awareness of the child or adolescent's state of mind or well being
may be limited or distorted. The discussion in this Monograph of
the work with children whose parents have been diagnosed with
the Munchhausen syndrome by proxy demonstrates a particularly

perverse way in which parents attempt to meet their own needs through the fabricated, or induced, physical illness of their children.

Gender may also influence the way in which the child or young person communicates his or her psychological distress and affect what is perceived to be a mental health problem. This is evidenced by the fact that boys are more likely than girls to be referred for conduct and attention-deficit disorders (Target & Fonagy, 1996). Furthermore, it seems that the deviant behaviour of young men may mask mental health problems, with some being detained inappropriately in the criminal justice system. Their depression or suicidal ideation may be hidden, the consequence of which can be tragic deaths in custody and in the community (Anderson & Dartington, 1998; Dwivedi & Varma, 1997). This may go some way to making sense of the high suicidal rates for boys (Shaffer & Piancentini, 1994). This suggests that adolescent psychiatric and psychotherapy services may neglect to meet the needs of young men who are psychologically distressed. Certainly the experience of the Cassel Adolescent Service is that young men with severe psychological difficulties are referred less often than are young women.

The dearth of appropriate mental health services for children and adolescents is also mirrored by the limited amount of research that has been undertaken on the effectiveness of different kinds of therapeutic work for this group. In the mid-1980s, the NHS Advisory Service investigated services for 12- to 19-year-olds and commented on the relative absence of evidence both of the incidence of psychological disturbance or of the effectiveness of treatment for adolescents (HAS, 1986). It seems that, almost twenty years on, this remains an underdeveloped area of research. Outcome studies on the effectiveness of psychotherapeutic treatment for children and adolescents are limited in comparison to the research that has been undertaken for adult patients. The case material presented in this monograph on the inpatient psychoanalytic treatment of children and adolescents may usefully add to this picture. The evidence that is available, however, appears to show that children and young people demonstrate clinical improvement with psychoanalytic psychotherapy in a range of contexts, and that this may be more acceptable to them than a cognitive-behavioural approach (Target & Fonagy, 1996).

Also, overall, there is little research on the treatment outcomes of different models of intensive family-based hospital treatment for children with severe emotional disturbance currently provided within the NHS. There is a paucity of systematically collected information about the clinical characteristics of these families, in terms of the range of social and psychological problems they bring to treatment and of data on the long-term outcome of different forms of treatment. Such research is complicated by the fact that there is a lack of agreement about what a "good" outcome might be for these families, and service providers differ considerably in terms of their implicit and explicit treatment objectives.

It is in light of this absence of outcome research that the Cassel Hospital is currently collaborating in a multi-centre evaluation study of hospital-based treatment of families and their children. The intention is that the data provided by this study will be useful to clinicians seeking to develop their treatment programmes and to referrers and commissioners who have to identify and purchase specialist services that will be most successful in their therapeutic work with these children.

While we know that children from very different social and cultural backgrounds can suffer from psychological distress, there are a number of risk factors that make some children and adolescents more vulnerable to mental health problems. In terms of their socio-economic background, those children and adolescents who are referred to mental health services are more likely to come from lone-parent households or reconstituted families, to live in poverty, and to be educationally disadvantaged (Audit Commission, 1999; Meltzer & Gatward, 1999). They are also likely to have a history of severe neglect, physical, sexual, or emotional abuse, and multi-agency involvement over a long period of time. This certainly accords with the family and social backgrounds of many of the children and some of the adolescents that we work with at the Cassel. The social and psychological experiences of these patients, and how they can be worked with therapeutically, is reflected in a treatment programme that focuses upon both the internal and the external worlds of the children or adolescents and their families.

As the chapters in this monograph illustrate, collaborative working relationships between the psychosocial nurse, the psychoanalytic psychotherapist, and the teacher in the therapeutic community milieu of the hospital are important. They enable clinicians to be mindful of the relationship between the external social and emotional functioning of the patient and his or her psychic world.

The importance of the multidisciplinary team, and the need for the child and parent to have their own psychotherapy, is discussed by Paul Coombe in chapter two and Deirdre Dowling in chapter three. Coombe details the psychoanalytic psychotherapy with a mother who had poisoned her two children and was diagnosed with Munchhausen syndrome by proxy. This shows, in a landmark case, the possibility of personality shifts in a parent with this diagnosis, which had previously been deemed "untreatable". Dowling discusses the psychotherapeutic work with a child, from a different family, who had been poisoned by her mother. Both authors demonstrate the importance of providing a therapeutic space in which the child and the parent can give voice to their experiences of being the abused or the abuser. Dowling argues that it is particularly important to enable the child to give expression to the emotional impact of the abuse. Coombe points out that joint supervision with the psychosocial nurse of the mother enabled him to be aware of how he might "annihilate the child from his awareness", a possible countertransferential response to the mother's hostility towards the child. It was also important to be aware of how the psychosocial nurse and adult therapist might form a couple and exclude the child psychotherapist, with the consequence that the child is no longer kept in mind. Dowling similarly charts how the dynamics of the treatment team can reflect the dynamics of the family being worked with.

As Dowling points out, much of the literature on Munchhausen syndrome by proxy itself excludes an exploration of the emotional impact on the child, focusing more on the abusing parent's own emotional and social deprivation in childhood. As was argued earlier, children's distress can often be rendered invisible or be overlooked by public services. Dowling argues that this covert act of abuse, which is carried out in the public arena, makes the failure to identify it even more distressing for the child who is being both cared for, but not cared for, by health professionals.

Dowling also notes that a central feature of Munchhausen syndrome by proxy is the lack of emotional containment in the family, with the consequence that feelings of need and hatred are acted out on the body of a child. This relationship between the mind and body is a clear theme running through the chapters in this Monograph, in terms of the child's or adolescent's emotional experience and of his or her behaviour.

In chapter four, Denis Flynn articulates the relationship between the various aspects of the inpatient treatment of children and their parents. He describes how the patient is held in treatment by the mutually cooperative effort of nurse and therapist and by the sustained involvement of patients and staff together in the therapeutic community. While the therapist and nurse each have their own roles and tasks, they can think and work together to provide some containment for each other. If conflict between workers occurs, a reflective staff process can help to turn it to therapeutic effect.

Flynn describes the therapeutic work with two severe child abuse family cases. In the first example, he examines the mother–infant sessions with the patient discussed in chapter two. The interactions between mother and child in the therapy sessions, and the observation and psychoanalytic understanding of the everyday interactions between the family, the nursing staff, and other patients in the community, were drawn together. This enabled the possible risks to the child, the effects on her development, and the nature and progress of the mother–child relationship to be assessed. Flynn shows that even with good motivation, negative and abusive patterns—repetitions of the core situations of abuse—become manifest within the treatment. Addressing key features of aggression and hatred towards the child actually contributes to therapeutic progress and, in particular, strengthens and makes more real the relationship between mother and child.

In the second example, Flynn focuses on the therapeutic work with a mother and her daughter, aged 2 years. In this family, a baby sibling had been killed by non-accidental injuries inflicted by the stepfather. Flynn shows how the trauma of early abusive events left their damaging mark on the surviving daughter and how the pain of still-current patterns of abusive relationships were experienced by the child. This case material demonstrates how multi-layered treatment that offers mother–child psychotherapy, individual child psychotherapy, and adult psychotherapy, together with intensive work in the hospital therapeutic community, can provide a crucible for the development of mother–child relationships.

In other cases, however, rehabilitation may not be possible or may be assessed as not in the best interests of the child. Throughout the assessment period, or intensive inpatient treatment of children and their families, keeping the emotional and physical safety of the child in mind is crucial. Child protection cases and formal inquiries have alerted us to the fact that practitioners may defend against the awfulness of child abuse, and the unconscious anxiety this produces, by engaging in what has been termed the "rule of optimism" (Dingwall, Eeklaar, & Murray, 1983); they focus on the positive aspects of parenting and deny the negative and harmful. Investing so much emotional and practical energy into the work can leave clinicians feeling emptied out when rehabilitation has not been possible. It may also put other patients in the community in touch with their own feelings of loss and abandonment. Making sense of these feelings, and working with them in the multidisciplinary team and the whole community, is vital to the collaborative nature of the relationships between staff and nurses working alongside patients.

Lee Marsden, in chapter five, provides a different but complementary perspective on the therapeutic work with children in the Cassel, reaffirming the importance of collaborative working. As we saw earlier, children referred to the mental health system may well be educationally disadvantaged. The Children's Centre provides education for children who are resident at the Cassel, and whose parents are inpatients in the Families Unit. Marsden articulates a particular way of working with these children that is both educational and therapeutic, and one that takes account of their emotional difficulties and learning needs. Drawing upon her work with two siblings, she describes the importance of the relationship between the emotional experience of the child and his or her capacity to learn. A balance needs to be struck between the learning task as defined by the curriculum and the need to adapt to the child's preoccupations and what they might be communicating, perhaps unconsciously, about the child's feelings.

This educational therapeutic work is provided in a protected space for the school-age children at the Cassel. In many ways it mirrors the "work of the day" in the more public areas of the therapeutic community environment, as the emphasis is on both playing and learning. What is particularly distinctive, however, is the attention devoted to the rhythm of the day for these children, and their attachments to parents, other patients, the staff in the centre, and the nurses and therapists in the wider hospital community. The detail of these relationships provides a rich source of material to make sense of the family dynamics and of the emotional life of the child, which itself aids the learning process. As we know, some children who have been emotionally, physically, or sexually abused may experience difficulties at school that may be defined as learning deficits, and their emotional needs are ignored or misunderstood. Marsden points out that by adopting an integrative perspective, learning can be both therapeutic and educational.

Many of the concepts that Marsden draws upon to articulate the therapeutic educational work with children at the Cassel are taken up in chapter six by Kevin Healy. These are the notions of transition, play, attachment, separation, dependency, and independence. Adolescence is a period of transition between childhood and adulthood and is a second phase of separation-individuation. It is a time fraught with different and transient emotions and states of mind, offering a particular kind of freedom to have new ideas and explore one's identity, as well as being marked by loss and grief and by defiance and dependence on parental figures. The shifting backwards and forwards between dependence and independence requires containing parental adults who can withstand this external and internal struggle, retain responsibility, and yet not impose a "false maturity" on their adolescent offspring.

Adolescence is likely to be a turbulent but normal phase of development that can be worked through when parents are themselves sufficiently contained and cared for. However, when the adolescent is exposed to a set of disturbed familial relationships and a social environment that do not provide sufficient containment, this transitional phase of life can become problematic. Just as the young person may fall between childhood and adulthood into a disturbed and frightening adolescence, he or she may also fall between the boundaries of child and adult mental health services and receive inappropriate or no therapeutic support.

Healy documents the kind of therapeutic inpatient work at the Cassel that is offered to older adolescents, aged 16 to 20 years, who have been identified as needing a particular kind of inpatient treatment, often when other kinds of support have failed. The different aspects of the treatment offer these young persons a new kind of milieu within which to explore their identity and their relationships with peers, substitute parental figures, and children younger than themselves, within the containing therapeutic structures of the hospital. They are given some responsibilities within the hospital to begin to develop a new separate identity, rather than the "false self" solutions described by Winnicott (1968b).

Healy, referring to Winnicott, points out that in adolescence identification with parents is rendered problematic as it is experienced as a "loss of personal identity". Being at the Cassel gives the adolescent the opportunity to explore this difficult issue of identification and how this has affected the development of his or her identity and personality structure.

Identification with, and hatred of, an abusive mother by an adolescent is the theme of chapter seven, in which Morice and McCluskey describe their therapeutic work with a young woman. They explore the painful process of adolescence for someone who has experienced loss and separation from male parental figures and abuse from mother. The psychosocial nurse and psychotherapist, as a therapeutic couple, had to withstand, in different ways, the patient's resistance to dependency feelings and her murderous feelings towards parental figures. The therapeutic couple—and, behind them, a reflective function within the whole adolescent team—provided an emotional container into which the unbearable feelings of the adolescent patient could be projected and made sense of. The setting of boundaries and limits in the hospital, and the ordinary work of the day in the community, also enabled the young woman to experience the concern of others and to have opportunities to repair what she felt she had destroyed.

In terms of this young person's disturbance, any separation was experienced as an abandonment, and loss was irreversible. As we saw earlier, adolescence is a time when issues of dependency and loss are struggled with, but for this young woman dependence on any adult figure had to be denied as a defence against the finality of loss. Furthermore, her concrete thinking, characteristic of those with severe borderline personalities, meant that she experienced separation and loss as a kind of death and felt that her own murderous wishes could kill. Phantasy and reality could not be distinguished, and her state of mind was often her state of body. This clinical material provides another illustration of the important relationship between mind and body during the transition of adolescence and how this can be distorted by the experience of abuse during childhood.

Both chapters seven and eight focus on the therapeutic work needed to contain "borderline" adolescents. Normal adolescence is a time of turbulence and evokes disturbing feelings, but it is also a time of hope and a love of life. For adolescents exhibiting borderline states of mind and behaviour, perhaps the hope in the treatment is that these can be worked with as a transient state of mind and social behaviour and not become fixed patterns of relating as adults. In chapter eight, Flynn and Turner explore the nature of the containment that is provided in the Cassel Adolescent Unit, drawing upon a number of case examples. Emphasis is placed on making sense of the adolescent's mental state and social behaviour and on finding a way to contain repetitious self-harming or suicidal behaviour and any temporary psychotic episodes, without the breakdown of the adolescent, within the structures of the therapeutic community. What is identified as crucial in inpatient treatment is an assessment of how the disturbance of the adolescent is manifested in the functioning of the adolescent group and the hospital community, and the impact of the adolescent on the community and of the community on the adolescent.

Earlier, reference was made to the process of detachment from parents and family that occurs during adolescence. However, for the adolescent patients at the Cassel the experience of living in the community, and being with peers, may offer them a sense of belonging and communality not previously experienced, however "troublesome" they may find this. Flynn and Turner describe how the relationships between the adolescents can enable a culture of empathy and cooperation, or antipathy, unresolved conflicts, and breakdown of social relationships, and that this needs to be made sense of.

Flynn and Turner make an important distinction between what they term the adolescent function and the borderline function—what is disturbing in an ordinary way for the adolescent and those around him or her, and what is pathological. The borderline adolescent will move between these two states, and it is crucial to be able to identify the shift between them. There is also a shift between paranoid-schizoid and depressive-position functioning in adolescence, but excessive projective identification and the confusion of internal and external reality is the hallmark of the "borderline function". Flynn and Turner argue that the move towards depressive-position functioning, characterized by the capacity to reflect thoughtfully about difficulties rather than blaming others, tolerate ambivalent feelings, and stay in touch with reality, are what all adolescents struggle with. They are building a new inner world and sense of value, and a sense of their new sexual body and identity. Flynn and Turner state that the attainment of this "sense of value" is the most important milestone of adolescence, but that it is fought against and hard won by borderline adolescents, for whom there is often a hatred of life and emotional knowledge. The value of the new sexual body or mind is attacked, perhaps by self-harm or suicide, depression, or drugs. By applying Bion's concept of the container and contained, Flynn and Turner explore through the case material how the receptive and emotional capacities of staff, in combination with the community living structures, provide the possibility for the borderline adolescent to develop a new sense of value.

Throughout the chapters in this Monograph, a sense of hope is held onto for the children and adolescents who are worked with at the Cassel. Flynn and Turner refer to the adolescent working towards a third position in the resolution of oedipal relations and taking their place in the outside world (Britton, 1989). In another way, the detail of the work of the multidisciplinary teams in the Adolescent and Families Services, and a "culture of enquiry", also

offers a third position (Foster, 1998) in which the conflicted relations between children or adolescents and their families can be
observed and thought about. A robust mental health system to
meet the needs of children and adolescents is also needed if hope
is to be sustained for their future lives.

CHAPTER TWO

The inpatient psychotherapy of a mother and child at the Cassel Hospital: a case of Munchhausen syndrome by proxy

Paul Coombe

T his account of the inpatient psychoanalytic psychotherapy of a mother and child at the Cassel Hospital is a case of Munchhausen syndrome by proxy. The mother brought two of her children to medical staff with complaints that were later found to be due to her chronic poisoning of them, which narrowly missed causing their death. It is an account of a treatment using both individual and group analytic methods in an inpatient psychoanalytic therapeutic community. Attention is drawn to the mother's use of projective identification defensively and malignantly in a concrete fashion, and its gradual conversion into a more benign agent. The function of the institution as a container is described, and comment is made on the experience of working with severe cases of child abuse.

Initial assessment

Ms Smith was referred to the Families Unit of the Cassel Hospital with her then several-months-old baby daughter, Jane, her third child, for assessment of their capacity to use the long-term inpatient psychoanalytic psychotherapy and psychosocial nursing in the hospital community. She was referred following a court case that led to her being placed on three years' probation as a result of her poisoning, by salt administration, her two older children, a boy of 5 years and a girl of 3 years.

This was a case of Munchhausen syndrome by proxy (Kennedy & Coombe, 1995; Meadow, 1977) in that she presented her children on numerous occasions to medical authorities claiming she had no knowledge of the cause of their illnesses. The poisoning was of a pernicious nature in that it continued surreptitiously over many months. Ms Smith was so convincing that local authorities were reported to have dug up pipes in the street looking for contamination of some sort. Eventually the children were taken to a casualty department, with one child unconscious and near death and the other also seriously ill. The two children were taken into care. During the admission itself, the mother's capacity to provoke anxiety throughout the institution was noted.

A typical Cassel Hospital Families Unit inpatient experiences a range of therapeutic inputs, most of which have been described in some detail by Kennedy, Heymans, and Tischler (1986). These include psychosocial nursing, individual psychoanalytic therapy for parents and children, group therapy for parents, and family sessions. School-age children attend the Children's Centre, which provides a social, educational, and psychotherapeutic milieu for the children. Patients are involved with other patients and staff through a complex range of formal and informal structures such as large community group meetings, gardening, cooking and so forth. Supervision of the nurse–therapist relationship enables the nurse, child therapist, and adult therapist to meet regularly, in the presence of a supervisor, to explore aspects of their developing relationship around the case. Psychodynamic attention to this relationship has been found to enhance the prognosis of such complex and difficult cases (James, 1984).

This account is written necessarily from the perspective of myself as psychotherapist of the mother, but it is important to understand that the formal psychotherapy was not the only active ingredient or, indeed, even perhaps the main one. From our first knowledge of the case, we had reservations about Ms Smith's treatment despite the Families Unit's developing expertise in managing child-abusing families. The social worker in charge of the case, an experienced and competent professional, had revealed that this case unnerved her more than any other in her twenty years' experience. We were concerned also to learn that some months prior to the referral, Ms Smith had to be legally held under section in a psychiatric hospital following her psychological de-composition at the time that she was separated from her youngest child, Jane. This child was conceived during the time that the events involving the two older children came to light.

An outpatient assessment was carried out when the family was referred for inpatient treatment. This revealed that Ms Smith had been raised in an interrupted fashion by her mother, grandmother, and stepfather and that she had been separated from her father at 10 months of age when he left the family. She had no further contact with him. We were denied details of Ms Smith's develop-mental history, partly because of the poor relationship between the Cassel and her mother and stepfather but also, perhaps, be-cause of the patient's facility for repressive denial. At the time staff were struck by her aloofness and incapacity to be emotionally in touch with the tragic set of events in which she had been involved. Nevertheless, a decision was made to offer a one-month inpatient assessment period to weigh up more accurately the prognostic factors, as she seemed committed to working to maintain the care and control of her youngest child. In such cases we were always uncomfortably aware that such individuals may continue to pro-duce children and repeat the cycle in some form or other down the generations unless something in the way of thorough-going inter-vention is achieved. From past experience we knew that in some cases even those who would ordinarily be considered unsuitable for long-term psychoanalytic psychotherapy on an outpatient ba-sis, due to insufficient ego strength, could benefit from inpatient treatment.

The inpatient assessment period

Ms Smith was a generally well-groomed young woman who talked in an immature and child-like fashion, sometimes with great rapidity. I remember my feelings of concern and anxiety beforehand because of all that I had learnt from other staff. During this first meeting she mentioned how she had recently said good-bye to her two older children (those she had poisoned), as she had begun to consider she would never again be thought capable of having full responsibility for their care. This left me feeling quite shocked, despite the fact that over the course of some days a growing desire to see them and eventually have full care of them was evident.

In therapy sessions during this period she frequently con-versed in a penetrating monotone on the topic of her estranged children. The theme seemed to be of her desire to have full care of her children again and to start to work on an improved mother–child relationship with them. There was, at times, rage expressed towards her husband and also the local social worker, both of whom were perceived as taking away her children or preventing her ready access to them. She seemed to have a strong need to deny her own role in bringing about a disruption of her relation-ship with the children. Instead, she projected onto others, who were perceived as the culprits. She acknowledged verbally the poisoning, but this seemed to lack a genuine feeling of responsibil-ity. In other words, she did not yet seem able to be in touch with her destructive urges towards her children and hence open the door to genuine remorse and reparation. She had a capacity to become enraged when her personal desires were thwarted, which was associated with an *inability to bear frustration*.

During this phase I learnt also that her maternal grandmother, to whom she had been very close, had died about one month prior to the birth of Ms Smith's first child, her son. From her description it seemed she harboured doubts that, in fact, the woman in the coffin at the funeral was her grandmother. This seemed to signal a difficulty in accepting the reality of loss. She was, however, soon devastated by grief even as she went into labour. The labour was complicated by a breech presentation, and further complications developed rapidly. During the labour a section of cord came down, necessitating a series of obstetric interventions. Subse-quently the baby was placed in a special care unit for several days, during which time Ms Smith did not see him. Following an early discharge from hospital, she recalled never really accepting that her son was her child. Thus the scene was set for the development of failure of bonding. I became aware of her intense jealous and envious feelings in relation to her husband's strong relationship with his mother and the two older children, a relationship that she wanted to destroy. At this early stage it seemed to me that possibly she could not bear others receiving what she had missed out on, and that such feelings may have contributed to her wish to kill her children, the objects of her husband's love.

She and her husband had been married several years, but the relationship had been unsatisfactory. This was partly because of what Ms Smith perceived as her husband's unduly happy involvement with his own family, which she experienced as being at her expense. Also, his employment took him away from home, often for several weeks to months. At these times she could feel desolate and isolated, especially with the responsibility of the children that she could not manage. By the time of her admission they had separated, and soon her husband met another woman who would eventually become his permanent partner, much to Ms Smith's chagrin. We did not have the opportunity to come to know the husband in any depth, partly because of the strength of the bitter feelings between husband and wife. Eventually they were divorced, and in time Mr Smith and his new partner gained care of the two older children.

At this early stage we became aware of massive splitting processes both within and outside the Cassel. Some workers were convinced that Ms Smith was dangerous, whereas others believed she had mainly good intentions. I also noted a peculiar absence of connectedness with herself. Though she talked endlessly of her three children, she herself often seemed absent. There seemed to be a lack of emotional relatedness with me, so much so that I could sometimes feel I could be any one of a number of anonymous figures. I was often left feeling that I did not matter to Ms Smith and that I was being used as a sounding board rather than as someone with whom she could relate person-to-person.

The child psychotherapist commented on what he called Ms Smith's "inconsequential coffee-morning talk" and lack of real emotional connectedness with others, including her daughter, Jane. On the other hand, a close and "clingy" quality of relation-

ship between mother and daughter was observed. The child psychotherapist considered that Ms Smith used her daughter as a
"comfort object" in that they normally slept together at night.

The nurse assigned to the family reported some observations
of genuine mutual pleasure between mother and Jane at bath-time
and on other occasions. There was also a controlling quality in the
way Ms Smith related to her and that it had been difficult for her
to find other patients to act in the supportive role of "night
contact" needed.

Overall, as the assessment period drew to an end there was
pessimism on the part of most staff, and we might easily have
expected that she and her daughter would be rejected for inpatient
treatment. Ms Smith seemed quite cut-off most of the time from
her actions with respect to her two older children and, by and
large, psychologically inaccessible despite certain islands of apparent higher functioning. In her last individual session prior to
an assessment meeting, in which all staff and external professionals involved would contribute their observations, I confronted her
strongly with the seriousness of her situation, including her role
in poisoning her children. This occurred in the context of her
continuing to scapegoat others for her own actions. This pressure
resulted in a change in her demeanour. She broke down and wept
and began to describe something of her childhood experience of
sexual abuse at the hands of a close male relative over a prolonged
period. It is difficult to convey the effect that this revelation had on
the staff as a group, but we all felt shocked and confused. This was
not because of the nature of the disclosure itself but our sudden
realization that perhaps she could use treatment to explore herself
and her actions after all. Part of the cataclysmic effect on staff
seemed to emanate from the fact that previously Ms Smith had
been so adamant, bigoted, and aloof but was now suddenly re-
vealing a vulnerable side. In retrospect, I suspected that this
disorganizing effect on the staff as a group might have been a
result of projective identification into us of her own confusion.
This may have been facilitated by ego-boundary weakness, sec-
ondary in part to her sexual abuse.

We decided to extend her assessment by a further few weeks.
This was an unusual decision at the Cassel but one that would
allow further investigation and examination of her claims and

exclusion of the possibility of her using such a claim to avoid culpability in relation to her children. This resulted subsequently in mother and daughter being accepted for treatment. The nature of her disturbance and the subsequent revelations of Ms Smith's experience of prolonged sexual abuse heralded what would be a feature of her admission—that is, our tendency to experience anxiety, horror, and awe.

The treatment—early phase (four months)

Ms Smith's tendency to control the sessions by expressing herself in a monotonous voice and generally restricting the range of the topics was uncomfortable to experience. Also I became acutely aware of her super-sensitivity to separation from her daughter. I began to suspect that this was not the common separation anxiety more typical of a neurotic disturbance but was related to a fear of collapse or disintegration. I began to wonder if Jane was needed to maintain her mother's personality integration and that such anxieties fuelled a relationship based on fusion.

Her first dream brought to therapy, about one month into treatment, was a mark of the state of her internal world at the time, despite the dream's brevity and sparse detail. In the dream *she was at the Cassel with her daughter, and her husband came to visit her. As they were talking he suddenly dropped dead in front of her as a result of spreading cancer.* She seemed to be unable to produce any associations, and so I, perhaps rather prematurely, suggested it might reflect a wish. She rapidly denied this but soon began to weep. She began to talk of her hatred of her abuser and the abuse, but as she spoke she experienced a sort of mental blackout or amnesic episode. This was characterized by fear and loss of recall of what she had just been talking about. This dream was important for several reasons. It was an expression of the intensity of the hatred she could feel towards those she was previously close to and, I suspected, an expression of her hostility also towards myself, as well as a fear of abandonment. More important, though, was the projection of advancing incurable and malignant destructiveness in the form of cancer into her husband. Also, I think that even at this stage there was a link with the nature of her attacks on her children, in the way of surreptitious poisoning: a slow seeping into their system of a destructive agent.

At about this time, she began to develop the rudiments of a capacity to feel concerned about her own mental state. She was beginning to be able to reflect on her intense and irrational anger with her son, whom she had seen on an access visit. She had experienced an impulse to hit him because of his incessant demands, which she felt as criticisms. I suggested that he may have reflected some unwanted aspect of herself, and this led her to recall her own mother's strong tendency to be critical and undermining of her as far back as she could remember. Her mother had needed her to be perfect, so she attempted to make *her* children perfect. She could not tolerate any messiness or untidiness by them. Also, at about this time, she was able increasingly to feel and express anger and even hatred of her mother. She wanted, at times, to extract a vicious revenge on both her mother and her husband. It was also at this time that she decided it would be best if she broke contact permanently with the two children she had poisoned. She presented, rather coldly, a rational argument as to why this should be so. However, I was struck more by the hostility and defensiveness betrayed by the decision, in that it seemed a readily available means of disavowing her murderous actions and simultaneously distancing herself from the experience of painful guilt. It also pre-empted the court's decision to remove the children from her care permanently.

About four months after her admission, she began a session talking of how she had seen me with one of my children outside the hospital and how shocked she had been by the experience. It led her to recall how, as a girl, she had a doll that she would sit on a chair and pour out abuse and anger at instead of facing her mother. It seemed that, up to this point, I had been identified with the doll, a passive, inanimate object, and also the helpless part of herself. She was identified with her mother, at least until the irrationality of this had been confronted by seeing me as a real and ordinary person outside the hospital. This seemed in accord with my past experience with her when I really could have been anyone or anything as far as she was concerned. I was then able to present something of this to her in the session. It seemed that she had a mother who could not contain or metabolize her psychological experience but would react, perhaps violently or abusively. At this time she also asked me how I felt about seeing her and what effect it had on me. I believe it was one of the first times she had glimpsed me as a real person with feelings, vulnerabilities, and perhaps the capacity for disgust—which, indeed, I could feel in relation to her and the poisoning of her children. It seemed a reflection of developing separateness from her objects. It was a time also marked by her developing a friendly relationship with an adult male patient, who was considered across the hospital as disturbed and capable of suicide or perhaps homicide or of becoming psychotic.

The nurse–therapist supervisions were of considerable use. These supervisions have the potential to reveal, for example, oedipal-derived rivalry and destructiveness in the interrelationships with hospital staff. Such dynamics may reflect issues in the family, and attention, at a supervisory level, can sometimes release a treatment from impasse. A not-uncommon situation is that of the adult therapist having annihilated the child from his or her awareness. This can be seen to be a reflection of the patient's hostility towards the child in certain cases. In this particular case, the nurse and I could form a couple that could exclude the child psychotherapist in some ways. This seemed a reflection of Ms Smith's psychopathological tendency to form tight and smothering relationships with objects based on envy, greed, and lack of individuation. Her nurse often felt drained by the patient's incessant demanding nature and expectation that the nurse had no other patients.

Middle phase (approximately twelve months)

This stage of her treatment was marked by a significant change in the structure of her psychotherapeutic experience as she started to attend a twice-weekly therapy group. This was to be in addition to one individual session with me; I was also the group therapist, with Ms Smith's nurse as co-therapist.

From the time of her entry into the group, Ms Smith was unenthusiastic about it. She reported that she found that the individual sessions provided her with considerable security, in contrast to the group, which made her feel threatened and on guard. During her early months in the group, I noticed that she began to experience and describe increasingly painful pangs of guilt in relation to the children she had poisoned.

During the latter half of her first year of treatment her daughter developed a series of chest infections associated with asthma, requiring multiple courses of antibiotics and necessitating ongoing paediatric management. Jane was noted by the child psychotherapist to be a regressed and unassertive child, whose mother frequently intruded into her space. There was concern that over several months mother and child had not been apart, so a regular fostering arrangement was set up, allowing each to have at least some time away from the other.

During this period, Ms Smith developed the firm desire to report her experience of sexual abuse to the police. This seemed both a reflection of a desire for revenge, as well as perhaps some growing capacity to bear the wrath of her family and of her mother in particular. A major development was when she made contact with her biological father, whom she had not seen since she was an infant. Following his desertion of the family he had remarried and had several children. Despite this he was eager to know his daughter and had a full and genuine appreciation of her difficulties. For the duration of her treatment he was an important resource, and he impressed staff as being a basically well-adjusted man, in contrast to Ms Smith's narcissistically disturbed mother. Ms Smith's mother had been found by staff to be critical, intolerant, and absolutely unable to experience guilt, remorse, or sadness in relation to her daughter's predicament. These qualities, of course, seemed reflected in Ms Smith's character. We could begin perhaps to consider that Ms Smith's mother had been unable to "contain" her daughter's painful feelings and instead experienced them as brutal attacks that demanded denial or retaliation.

Prior to her entry into the group, Ms Smith had come to imagine herself and me in an exclusive and cloistered relationship, so much so that she once commented humorously, but half seriously, that she thought I lived in my consulting-room only waiting for her. This fantasy seemed to reflect the nature of many relationships in her life, past and present, most notably that with her daughter Jane. It seemed to me that she fused with others in relationships, unable to bear separation because of the fantasy of losing a part of herself and ultimately fragmentation.

During this middle phase of her therapy, I became increasingly aware of her inability to mourn the loss of her children and the estrangement from her mother. There was a strong tendency for her to use new relationships outside the hospital, such as that with her rediscovered father and a boyfriend, to diminish the current experience of loss. Nevertheless, as the psychotherapeutic and psychosocial work continued, there was a progressive and qualitative development of the capacity to experience loss. While I was on leave during the summer of her first year of treatment, she became quite deeply depressed for the first time during her admission, with some rudimentary capacity to connect this in her mind with my absence and that of the child psychotherapist. At Christmas-time, some twelve months after admission, she experienced genuine sadness associated with the loss of her children and her poisoning of them. This remorse was both deep and persistent. The stable and secure hospital environment for her, at the time, also seemed to stimulate memories of her childhood, specifically the relative absence of a warm, safe, and happy home and relationship with a mother. Increasingly she seemed able to bear remorse and guilt without evacuating the experiences into the environment.

As the months progressed she became an active member in the group, able to confront appropriately and challenge others in a constructive fashion. She came to see aspects of herself in others and obviously struggled with these split-off parts of herself reflected in others. The containing nature of the institution and the therapy were allowing a progressive integration. For example, when instances of child abuse were discussed in the group, Ms Smith would rise to her full height and admonish such mothers for abuse of their children. This tendency to self-righteousness diminished as she was confronted in the group about her role with her children.

An important development was the emerging tendency to see me as a persecutor. Early on in her treatment she related to me in a sweetly innocent and benign fashion that made me feel uncomfortable. However, more and more she reacted to me, mainly in group sessions, as a persecutor. It seemed that in the transference there was real confusion between the helpful, constructive, good therapist/mother and the nasty, wilful and destructive therapist/ mother.

She frequently had strong reactions to the arrival of new members into the group and tended to remain withdrawn and silent for some sessions after such an event. As time proceeded, however, she became able to make use of interpretations relating to her hatred of the arrival of new siblings and recalled how jealous she had been when her mother was pregnant and went on holiday, leaving her at home. She spoke of her deep bitterness towards her younger sister, the product of her mother's second marriage, who seemed to be the apple of her parents' eyes, in contrast to the ugly-duckling image of Ms Smith. Another event of significance about one year after admission was the entry into the group of a man who had been admitted with his wife and their daughter whom the mother had attempted to poison. This was a major event for everyone in the group, but especially Ms Smith. As well as issues of identification with the poisoning mother, she reacted bitterly towards her husband because of his maleness and was reminded of her experience of sexual abuse. Over many months she was able to develop a reasonable relationship with him despite her initial identification of him with her sexual abuser. This developed through repeated interpretation and confrontation of the various aspects of the identification.

She sometimes spoke of the strangeness of having my co-therapist—her nurse—and me in the group together with her. Sometimes it seemed to make her feel uneasy, at other times she described it as an added security in the face of the tumultuous dynamics of the institution. She, more than any other patient in the group over two years, some fourteen in all, found it most difficult to entertain fantasies about us as a couple. Perhaps this said something of her fears as a child in considering what her parents' private relationship was like, or of her jealousy and envy of the parental couple. The others in the group could more readily describe in some way their usually humorous fantasies about us which sometimes included sexuality, but Ms Smith frequently said there just weren't any at all so how could she talk about them. Nevertheless, as the treatment proceeded, she became more able to consider this aspect, although mostly with a certain degree of disdain. We were frequently aware of her greedy desire to keep us all to herself and her difficulty in sharing us with others in the group.

Early in the second year of treatment, rehabilitation was begun formally. This meant that a flat was found locally for her, and she was able to prepare for the eventual discharge from the Cassel. Soon it was agreed that she could spend increasingly longer periods at home, on some weekends, with Jane. At about this time, in an individual session, she reflected on having been in the hospital for about one year, reviewed the past, and came to consider her motives for poisoning her two children. It was a session marked by uncharacteristic honesty and insight. She said: "I now know that I wanted to destroy my children . . . to kill them. . . . I couldn't stand them any more." I asked her why she thought she had poisoned the children. She considered the question thoughtfully and said she thought it was a means of attacking her mother. She recalled that as a girl she frequently wanted to destroy things after conflict with her mother. She recalled a phone call with her mother two weeks previously after which she went down to the Thames near the hospital and seriously considered drowning herself. This had been a real and worrying event in the hospital. She detailed how, as a girl, after arguments with her mother she would often break a valued and loved possession, and she specifically recalled a much-loved hand-mirror. My subsequent interpretation drew attention to the wish to destroy her mother in herself and in the various reflections of herself in the mirror and especially in her children, and, furthermore, that she wanted to break her mother into fragments, as she herself felt after arguments.

Some seventeen months into treatment, in the course of an individual session, I used the term "being rid of" in relation to how she dealt with her children: perhaps a slip on my part. I suggested she may have had a fantasy that in being rid of her children she may have rid herself of some badness but that, in fact, such a hated part of herself might still reside within her and could be explored usefully. This allowed her to attack me angrily and then get up to leave the room. This was her mother's view, she said, and she did not "get rid of" her children at all, and so on. I suggested she had turned me into her cruel and rejecting bad mother. What seemed to occur was a lodging in me of a harshly critical and persecutory part of herself, an aspect of her superego, to which she could then direct hate and wish to rid herself of by leaving the room. She went on to describe her sense of inadequacy with her children throughout their infancy and how she was criticized by her mother and husband. It seemed that she projected her self-critical agency into the children, which she could only distance herself from by killing them.

It is important to appreciate that the sequence I have just described, of her causing irritation in others who then attacked her, allowing her to respond with rage, occurred frequently in her relationships throughout the hospital. This manifestation of projective identification could be interpreted in the therapy sessions as confrontation of her characteristic way of relating. Interestingly, the session just described was terminated ten minutes prematurely by myself through a parapraxis, and a minute after she had left the consulting-room she returned, pointing out my error with some glee. Subsequently we had the remainder of the session. This allowed me to make some comment about what I had been left with that perhaps I could not bear, allowing a glimpse of the painful feelings that the therapist and other staff members were attempting to contain in dealing with her (Bion, 1959).

For some months she developed a relationship with an easy-going man outside the Cassel that became sexual and seemed very satisfying for her. However, she became troubled by thoughts that he was too good for her. This caused her considerable discomfort, eventually causing her to end the relationship. It seemed that she needed an external persecutor and that without such a figure in her life her internal persecutor became more active.

Later phase of therapy (approximately four months)

Somewhat later in the year she began to experience fantasies of seeking out her mother to express love for her. This led me to suggest that she could envisage and wanted to find a loving part of her mother. She came also to reflect wistfully on how she had taken into herself so many of the bad aspects of her mother, rather than the good and loving mother that she could imagine also existed. She reflected on how difficult it would be to leave the hospital with her daughter at the end of her treatment. She would be leaving me, her nurse, and the child psychotherapist, as well as the hospital community. She had come to feel that these were fundamentally good influences in her life. Increasingly she became more able to experience and express genuine gratitude. She began to come to sessions wearing a mini-skirt to make herself sexually attractive for me. She could accept that she was less threatened by me as a sexual object and was more able to use sexual interpretations in a manner that had previously been impossible. She became able to have a disagreement with certain individuals without the conflict descending into a character assassination and could more easily continue a relationship with the individual afterwards.

Some four months before discharge she reported the following dream. *She was walking along a road with a nurse from the Cassel—not her nurse, however—and as she walked she passed a paddock with cows grazing. She continued to walk and finally came to a coffee shop, and a female patient friend of hers was there. However, she kept walking and arrived at a pub with the nurse. In this pub were three Dr Coombes talking with each other, and she was quite shocked.* She laughed at her recollection of the dream and suggested that I was multiplying as though it were an outer-space movie—there were so many of me. At this stage my only comment was to suggest I might seem a persecutory and all-pervasive figure from whom she could not escape. Immediately she reported a second dream in which *she woke up pregnant, holding her abdomen.* She could readily see her unconscious wish for a baby, despite consciously not wanting one, even though she had been sterilized. She came back to the earlier dream and continued to reflect on it. She considered that the cows in the paddock represented other Cassel patients being fed and feeding each other while she remained somewhat aloof. The nurse walking with her was seen as a support. As for the three Dr Coombes, she wondered if they related to the three other patients on the unit who were in therapy with me at that time. They were seen as rivals with whom she had to share me while struggling hard to suppress her jealousy. Also, I was able to suggest that it might say something of her intense need for me. After the session I thought that the cows may have represented her fragmented mother from whom she could never really receive a satisfying feed, and also her fragmented self which was unable to provide a good feed for others. This dream, and its significance for her, preoccupied her in several subsequent individual and group sessions in terms of how she warded off and controlled her hateful and jealous feelings towards others.

Frequently we were aware of her need to split her objects into idealized and hated parts, and I used opportunities as they arose to challenge this adjustment. Relatively late in the therapy she discussed her maternal grandmother in an idealized fashion and how she wished she had been with her to protect her. She contrasted her grandmother with her awful mother, and this allowed me to suggest the possibility that her grandmother was perhaps not so perfect because Ms Smith had not been able to tell her of the sexual abuse. I suggested that this might indicate something lacking in the relationship. She became angry with me, and this soon became a rage. I said that there might be a fear that if she admitted to her consciousness a flaw in her grandmother, then the wholly good view of her would collapse. She remained very angry with me, saying, how could I say such things, and anyhow her grandmother had been ill for years. She believed the news would kill her, and if she died, she would have no one. By this stage I felt thoroughly guilty but managed to say that she had turned me into a bad therapist in her mind. I added that she seemed to need to keep the good and bad apart in different individuals and that it was difficult for her to consider that her mother, grandmother, therapist, and others were more likely to be a mixture. She left the session ten minutes early, loudly slamming the door! I decided not to notify staff about this session but to see how she managed as it was quite late in her treatment and it seemed a crucial prognostic test. As the Cassel is a therapeutic community, it is sometimes helpful for the therapist, or indeed other staff, to share with others in the treatment team the likelihood of impending crises. In fact, she managed well and quickly reintegrated and was able to work in subsequent sessions.

Towards the time of discharge I had a short holiday and, on my return, in a group session she gave me a "stick of rock" that she had bought while she herself had been on a holiday. Subsequently, back in the first individual session after the break, she said she was proud of how she had coped without me and, in fact, did not miss me, but this was said in rapid talking style, suggesting denial. Also, of course, she and her daughter were soon to be discharged. She talked about the "stick of rock" and laughingly indicated that she had hostile fantasies that the "E-numbers" or additives in the "rock" would make me jump around and become hyperactive. I suggested the "rock" might unconsciously be a way of opposing the urge to attack me as she had poisoned her two children through oral means. She then mentioned that a female co-group member had suggested to her that the "rock" may be a phallic symbol. This allowed me to suggest the idea that the gift might indicate in her unconscious a wish for me to penetrate her sexually. This embarrassed her and caused her to deny the idea, but she followed this by recalling that just before my holiday in a session with me she had been curious about my lovemaking with my wife. I suggested this might also be a defended way of wondering about her and me making love. (Possibly this reflected a means of holding on to a satisfying relation with me.) She became mildly annoyed with me, saying I had not appreciated the gift and she would never give me anything in the future. However, the session developed with further discussion of her desire to ward off and not acknowledge hateful feelings towards me for deserting her by going on leave, and her fears of how she would cope after discharge.

Towards the end of treatment the child psychotherapist commented that Jane's development was proceeding well and that the mother–child relationship was characterized by genuine warmth and appropriate connectedness. There were, however, some concerns about the degree of institutionalization in the pair. Ms Smith requested referral for ongoing psychotherapy on an outpatient basis and preferred this to be with a female therapist, and a referral was made (but subsequently not taken up). We considered this quite a positive move because there was no statutory need for this to occur. She had become able to reflect with concern on her daughter's experience of imminent departure from the Cassel, their home for nearly two years. This seemed to be based on an empathic and intuitive appreciation of her daughter's position as well as an awareness of her own conflicted state.

Nevertheless, her destructive side was expressed at discharge because she refused to participate in a research programme involving interviews with a research psychologist, something she had participated in throughout the admission. This research was seen not unrealistically, for a time at least, as a means of helping to ensure the future survival of the Cassel.

Discussion

Retrospectively my attention has been brought to consider the unusual experience of working with individuals and families in the context of the severe abuse and even death of children. Such events touch at the core of us all and can provoke anti-therapeutic reactions in professionals. To work effectively with such cases we must have considerable experience and a personal and intellectual framework for support. The horror itself can be seductive and fascinating, and maintaining a focus on the therapeutic task by the support of a strong institution and the relationships and structures within it are essential. In that sense, the existence of such an institution as the Cassel becomes not a luxury but a basic prerequisite for such work to be carried out despite all its difficulties, shortcomings, and cost.

The case is interesting for many reasons, not the least being that it may be a rarely documented example of toxic concrete actions that parallel psychic projective identification. Initially, she forcefully and violently evacuated poisonous and bad contents. These projections appeared to be a vain unconscious hope of retaining within herself sustaining and good aspects. After admission to the Cassel, these forceful psychological projective identifications invaded those around her in the institutional, group, and individual setting. Frequently, this aroused hostility in others and a subjective experience of being forcefully controlled. Ms Smith's pre-oedipal orientation gave way as time went on to oedipal/sexual preoccupations. The "stick of rock" episode demonstrates a more benign use of projective identification in that hostile and loving impulses perhaps were fused. Finally, towards the end of her admission, there seemed to be glimpses of a loving capacity, enabling her to communicate better with others in terms of empathy and intuition.

A fundamental and vital feature of the Cassel treatment for Ms Smith, and indeed for any patient, is the provision of containing structures. These are multiple, and they extend far beyond the therapist–patient relations. It includes the existence, on a daily basis, of relationships of differing quality with groups and individuals allowing the holding and evolution of conflictual states of mind.

Ms Smith seemed to have an uncontrollable capacity to invade others in an attempt to destroy the goodness in them, and this was displayed throughout her treatment but in a steadily diminishing fashion. Such a capacity, mediated via projective identification, may be based upon envy (Klein, 1957). Throughout her admission she frequently seemed to attack and belittle others who demonstrated characteristics that were constructive and which the patient did not possess. One suspects from the history and the transference–countertransference that this was complemented by her experience of a mother who was similar and who was also unable to contain her destructive attacks as an infant. It is interesting to consider to what degree her early experience determined a more destructive outcome of the sexual abuse—for example, in terms of her inability to bring the abuse to an end more rapidly, destroying the potential for a more normal adolescence. The eventual psychological outcome of sexual abuse in general will be very much influenced by the pre-existing internal world already determined in infancy.

CHAPTER THREE

Poison glue:
the child's experience
of Munchhausen syndrome by proxy

Deirdre Dowling

This chapter examines the emotional impact of Munchhausen syndrome by proxy on a 6-year-old child who at a younger age had been poisoned by her mother. It describes the child's treatment in child psychotherapy over twenty months at the Cassel Hospital, where the family worked towards her successful rehabilitation home. The work with her showed her experience of dangerous relationships in her family that left her distrustful of any new relationship and doubtful of her capacity to be close without being destructive. Like her parents, she was terrified of facing the murderous feelings in the family, retreating into denial when life was too painful. This chapter describes three phases of treatment: fear of separation and preoccupation with the trauma of poisoning, ambivalence about facing the destructiveness in the family, and the move into more appropriate latency behaviour as she prepared to go home with her parents. It concludes with an overview of the impact of Munchhausen syndrome by proxy on the developing child, as shown in this treatment. Consideration will be given to the delay in emotional and cognitive development, the interference with the capacity to relate, the retreat into illness under stress, and the fear of permanent damage caused by the emotional and physical abuse.

Loretta

Loretta was poisoned by her mother when she was 4 years old. Her mother admitted giving her overdoses of medication while Loretta was in hospital being investigated for vomiting. This event was then linked with many other unexplained illnesses and injuries. Her father denied knowledge of the abuse. Loretta was the victim of Munchhausen syndrome by proxy, a condition in which a seemingly caring parent takes her child to the doctor for the treatment of fabricated symptoms or an induced serious illness. In this chapter, I describe Loretta's treatment in psychotherapy at the Cassel Hospital, where I saw her in twice-weekly therapy over twenty months. This treatment was only possible in the context of intensive inpatient work with the whole family, but I focus here on my work with the child, exploring the emotional impact of Munchhausen syndrome by proxy and the slow process of recovery.

When I began seeing Loretta, I tried to imagine the effect that this poisoning would have on a child who is old enough to understand that, while pretending to help her get well, her mother was poisoning her. How would this perversion of mothering and caring affect her view of herself and her capacity to relate to others? Later in therapy Loretta used the image of *poison glue* to describe her own attempts to attack our relationship, and this image remained in my mind as a powerful description of the dangerous attachments she had experienced in her family. She was suspicious and distrusting of any relationship and of her own capacity to be close without being destructive. Another important theme was Loretta's denial of her parent's hatred and murderous behaviour, often preferring a smudged view of the world to the pain of seeing clearly. Much of the therapeutic work revolved around this conflict within a growing capacity to see, think, and understand her experience.

Reviewing the current literature on Munchhausen syndrome by proxy, in order to compare this child's experience with others,

I found that most of the work focused on the parents, attempting to understand their pathology. These papers emphasize the abusing parents' own deprivation in childhood and their need for care (Loader & Kelly, 1996; Schreier, 1992). What is less clear is the abusing parent's view of the child, hidden behind the façade of concern—that is, whether the parent has the capacity to see the child as a separate person. When the abuse is discovered, there is less said about the child's perspective, perhaps because many of the children are pre-verbal. In chapter four, Denis Flynn examines both the mother–infant relationship in a family where the siblings had been poisoned and the emotional effect on the child. Turning to the wider literature on child psychotherapy with children who have been abused, there are common theses that are relevant. Juliet Hopkins (1986) looks at children who have been subject to repeated trauma. She describes their need to deny parents' responsibility for the injuries, preferring to blame themselves. She suggests two explanations: the children's loyalty to their parents and wish for them to be perfect, and their need to deny their vulnerability. "The child prefers to feel responsible for, even guilty about an external situation which she or he can control within the ambit of his omnipotence, rather than admit his helplessness in the face of any intolerable reality" (1986, p. 70).

A preoccupation with trauma and inability to learn or get on with life is also common in abused children. What is different about Munchhausen syndrome by proxy, compared with other forms of child abuse, is the covert infliction of illness on the child by the parents. This covert act often happens in a public arena that makes the failure to discover it much more distressing, for the child is near help but unable to get it. Herbert Schreier (1992) describes the shock and incomprehensibility of this act for workers. So much more must be the impact on the child who faces continual uncertainty and fear of repeated abuse, which has to be survived alone.

Inpatient treatment at the Cassel Hospital

A brief description of the work of the Cassel Hospital may be useful here, as this provided the containing structure that made possible the individual work with the child. The hospital has three units, one for adults, one for adolescents, and one for families. In the Families Unit, the whole family is admitted for inpatient treatment. Families live as part of a therapeutic community with the adults and adolescents. Patients share responsibility for the daily management of the hospital with the nurses. Individual families have their own nurse who supports them with the difficulties of daily life. The children's safety is paramount, and families are closely monitored, particularly in the early phases of treatment. Both adults and children have individual therapists who, with the nurse, form the treatment team around the family. The nurse–therapist team will meet the whole family together on a regular basis, integrating the treatment of the individual with that of other family members, and trying to make sense of the family's life together. Children go to school or nursery in the hospital until they are able to manage again in a local school. It is the combination of psychosocial nursing, individual, marital, and group therapy, and living as part of a community that provides the intense holding experience for a family in distress. In each of these settings, patients are encouraged to think about their experience, rather than act on impulse or retreat. The emphasis is on managing ordinary events and supporting the functioning aspects of families in treatment (Kennedy, 1997).

For a child psychotherapist, working in a residential setting like this is a very different experience from working in the community. I see the children about the building every day and hear about the family from nurses and therapists throughout the week. If there are safety issues concerning the child, I can be drawn into a management role alongside the nurses, setting clear limits with the parents about their behaviour, and this can feel uncomfortable alongside my therapist role. It is easy to feel bombarded with too much information about the child's external world and lose the important preoccupation with his or her inner reality and conflicts. I have to filter what information I give to the treatment team about the sessions to protect confidentiality, while sharing enough to support the work. Every therapist finds his or her own way of adapting his or her technique to the setting, and it can often feel an uneasy compromise. What is gained is the support and containment of close working as a team that makes it possible to deal with the intense anxiety of the work, particularly where severe abuse has occurred.

Working with severely disturbed families, adults, and adolescents in a residential setting like the Cassel creates severe stresses in the staff team which, if left unresolved, would make the work unmanageable. Over the years, the Cassel has developed structures that support the staff by enabling them to process the feelings that occur within themselves and between them. Typically, the treatment team can reflect the dynamics of the family they are working with, so there can be powerful splits between the mother's therapist and the child's, or one of the therapists and the family's nurse, each identifying with particular aspects of the struggle and conflict in the family members. Lydia Tischler (1986) describes one technique that has been developed for monitoring the nurse–therapist relationship. A senior nurse and therapist who are not involved with the family directly meet with the treatment team about once every six weeks to think about their work with the family. They "pay special attention to the feelings in the countertransference which patients inevitably evoke in their treaters, and the effect these feelings have on their work" (p. 95). In a weekly "strains" meeting, a similar process occurs within the whole staff community, monitoring how the staff group is mirroring the strains of the patient community. Nurse meetings and unit meetings occur almost daily and continue this processing so that connections can be made between the ordinary functioning of the family and the understanding of the conflicts that are emerging in therapy. Often a small event, like a parent–child conflict over food at mealtimes, will illuminate a dynamic in the family that contributed to the breakdown in parental care. It is this multi-layered approach that helps make sense of the complex pathology in many families we work with and creates a safe setting for the work. An area of tension or dysfunction missed in one aspect of treatment will usually show itself in another in a slightly different form.

For Loretta's family, where isolation and secrecy had been a way of life, living as part of a therapeutic community offered the opportunity to manage things in a different way. Loretta was admitted to the Cassel with her family several months after the diagnosis of Munchhausen syndrome by proxy. She had been in foster care since the discovery of her abuse. The aim was to assess whether rehabilitation was possible and, if so, to offer treatment to the family towards this goal. Loretta would continue to spend weekends at the foster home until the outcome was clear. If the process was not successful, an adoptive family would be sought for Loretta.

Beginning treatment: is it safe to separate?

It was hard to establish a relationship with Loretta. Although she readily befriended new people, it was the superficial clinging contact of a deprived child. I recall my first impression of her when she began psychotherapy, a slight awkward little girl with thick smudged glasses that dominated her face. In her first therapy session, she readily left her mother, with a big hug.

> Loretta wanted me to know how grown up she was, writing letters and numbers. She began to play, asking me to be a child, while she was an angry mother who was cross with my naughtiness. She then became a nice mother who called me darling. Loretta alternated between these two roles, becoming increasingly frantic in her play. She told me about her dreams of dragons and monsters, telling me to pretend I was a child having nice dreams of dolphins who cuddled me. Just before the end, she became the dragon who ate me and both her parents. When I asked if she was worried I might become this frightening monster she quickly agreed, then put away her things, apparently cheerful, and returned to her mother.

I was surprised by Loretta's openness in this first session when she showed me so clearly her conflicting experience of her mother, both loving and angry, her nightmare fears of dragons and monsters, and her hungry deprivation. The anxiety about facing these difficult feelings, denied in our first meeting, came out in the following sessions when Loretta refused to leave her mother and come alone, kicking and screaming once she was in my room. When she did feel safe enough to remain alone, she began to re-enact scenes of her poisoning and recounted frightening dreams where mothers and teddy bears were killed and eaten by dragons.

Outside the session with me she was very disturbed, with severe temper tantrums and nightmares. She was unable to learn in school, preoccupied with playing out the same scenes of the hurt baby. Despite the intense distress Loretta showed in her behaviour, I felt strangely detached from this young girl and I thought this must mirror her profound distrust of me. She could show me what was wrong but she had no expectation that I could offer warmth or concern.

For the first few months of treatment, I found Loretta's sessions distressing and difficult to understand. She communicated more openly in her behaviour in the community, showing us how frightened and angry she was. For example, she had to return to the hospital where she had been poisoned by her mother, to have an operation on her eye to correct a squint. She managed the hospital stay well, but afterwards she regressed, provoking me by causing chaos in my room and battling for control with her parents. They were unable to set limits to her behaviour, absorbed in their own needs and concerns. She told a nurse that her parents had given her tablets again, and we became very anxious about her safety. When this was investigated, the allegations seemed unlikely to be true. We thought Loretta was letting us know how dangerous it felt to be in her family and that she was terrified she might be abused again. This distrust was reflected in her relationship with me. She often refused to stay alone, and, when she did, she reversed roles, insisting that *she* was the therapist in charge and I the vulnerable child.

I recall feeling overwhelmed at this time. I wondered if there was any basis for Loretta to establish a different relationship with her parents or her therapist, since she felt such profound distrust and fury resulting from the abuse. I wondered whether Loretta should return to her foster home and give up the idea of rehabilitation, as an easier and safer option. I imagine my countertransference feelings reflected her hopelessness about the task ahead. To balance this, Loretta was able to make use of her sessions. She showed a wish for safe boundaries to contain her fury by putting the crocodile inside fences, telling the baby it was not safe otherwise. This suggested some hope that psychotherapy might be helpful, offering her a contained space to articulate her confused and painful feelings.

In this phase of treatment, both I and the other workers found it difficult to process the primitive feelings aroused by this family and to distinguish between fantasy and reality. We needed our colleagues, helpfully distanced from the family's projections, to help us think about these powerful feelings.

In time Loretta was able to use her sessions to make sense of the anxiety, anger, and fear that were too shattering to think about when they occurred. She introduced a fireman and policeman into her play, showing her need for a benign authority within herself and her family. She also told me about the judge who had not let her return home after she was given tablets because it was not safe. I thought she was beginning to recognize that her abuse resulted from her parents' failure to control their feelings and that she, also, could become overwhelmed in the same way when she felt there were no limits. This enabled her to achieve some feelings of separateness from her parents with the recognition of the difficulties they faced. Sorting this out seemed to make it possible for her to begin to learn, and she showed me proudly at the end of one session how she could add up and do sums.

Loretta's growing attachment to me, and the separation anxieties it evoked, recalled earlier memories of the painful separation from her parents when she was taken into foster care. I realized that, to Loretta, removal into foster care had been as traumatic as the abuse and had confirmed her feelings of rejection by her parents.

The next three months: is it safe to look, to see?

Loretta's growing ability to think about her experiences led to a painful conflict as to whether it was bearable to look at the feelings of hatred in her family, particularly between herself and her mother. She became more enraged by her parents' denial and the ignorance of the other adults around that had left her in continual danger. She felt that their denial had made it impossible for her "to see" and understand the physical and emotional distress she had to suffer.

The event that precipitated this phase of work was Loretta's mother's miscarriage in the fourth month of treatment. Like all other important issues in this family, this pregnancy had been kept secret until denial was impossible. It was clear that Loretta was aware of her mother's pregnancy, although she had not been told about this by her parents. Alongside anxiety about her mother's health and feelings of exclusion, the miscarriage re-evoked Loretta's fear of secrets in the family. This became clear in her next session, when Loretta was furious that I had been as ignorant of her parents' evasion as other professionals had been in the past. She told me, "You're blind. I can see." She was also angry that I was going on holiday. Loretta was dismissive of her parents, depicting them in her play as two needy people who go off to the teddy for a hug and a kiss, leaving the baby alone crying. At the same time, she was frightened by her anger and the devastation it caused internally, as shown by the following two sessions:

> Loretta began pretending she was a monster, throwing the teddy on the floor and kicking him. I had to be a frightened daughter. The scene changes. It is night and Loretta is now a frightened baby daughter who tries to comfort herself with "dolphin dreams". She wakes her mother who is angry, and "the carpet is full of nails". Loretta pretends to pick up the nails and then tells me the room is safe.

> In the next session, just before my leave, Loretta returned to the night scene, but this time the baby kills the mother, then cries because she is alone. Loretta as the baby then kills herself and shatters her glasses. She lies there for a long time, sad and desolate.

I felt shaken by Loretta's despair and loneliness in these sessions. Now that she could allow herself to feel her fury, she was frightened by its intensity and her wish to murder the hateful parent who does not comfort her. Her rage was initially in response to my blindness, then my impending holiday, which deprived her of comfort and a place for understanding. In her murderous rage, she retaliated and killed her mother figure, then killed herself, destroying the glasses that represented her growing capacity to see the painful reality of her own destructiveness as well as that of her parents.

Loretta was more frightened of her anger because her mother often became ill and she felt responsible. Now that Loretta was no longer used to exhibit illness on behalf of her mother, we could see how her mother used illness and requests for medical investigation to gain attention for herself. Munchhausen syndrome by proxy had become straightforward Munchhausen syndrome. She was booked to go to hospital for one of these investigations during my next holiday, so Loretta felt she was being abandoned by both her mothering figures. Loretta's concern for her mother became confused with her anger and wish to retaliate. She told me stories of mothers dying in hospital. Once again she became locked into battles with her mother and unable to leave her to come to her session.

On my return from leave, her mother was still in hospital and Loretta refused to leave her father, so I suggested that he sit in the room with her until she could let him go. She was very regressed, wetting her pants, wanting to bite me, wishing to be in control. However, she was able to use the familiar structure and thinking space of the session to recover her capacities, and, by the next session, she was able to come alone and work out her feelings of uncontainment and rejection in symbolic play. The theme was clear. I was the bad mother who had given her the wrong clothes and a broken cot and hurt her in the head. During the break Loretta had found it hard to hold on to her still fragile sense of self without the external support of therapy. By the end of the session, she showed her wish for closeness, again pretending to be a baby who wanted to share a bed with me. When I saw Loretta next, she reacted against this vulnerability, pretending she was a grown-up who did not need a mother, who could care for herself and her baby. This may also have been a reaction to her parents' recently collapsed state. As she justifiably complained: "I can't cuddle myself." Alongside feelings of anger, and pessimism, Loretta also began to show some confidence in her own strengths, trying to construct in her play a new home for her family.

It was now eight months into treatment. Loretta knew that soon a decision would be made about rehabilitation, and this would entail saying goodbye to her foster-mother whom she continued to see almost every weekend. Her anxieties about the risks of returning to her "old" home, as she called it, and her fury at the idea of eventually losing me began to appear in her sessions. She pictured herself as an owl that would keep watch all night to keep her home safe, showing the vigilance she still felt was necessary. She was caught in a conflict between her anxiety and love for her parents. Struggling with this, she stopped caring for herself and once again she came to sessions with smudged glasses, which almost got carelessly broken, although they did not need repair as they had done on the previous occasion. When another family's treatment broke down, and the daughter returned to foster care, Loretta became more in touch with her wish to remain with her mother and she turned to her for comfort. Her mother was able to respond with genuine warmth to Loretta's wish for closeness, and I felt a little more hopeful about the future of their relationship.

Is this a dangerous game? The question of rehabilitation

Loretta was beginning to mature. She was becoming more independent, able to come to sessions alone, and she was making progress in school. At the same time, she was worried that her parents would not be able to manage her difficult behaviour if she returned home with them. She began testing my watchfulness in her sessions with risky gymnastics, as if to check whether I could keep her safe. She talked of "old times", her old school where she had been unhappy and the sick baby who was better now but might get ill again. In her games, I had to be a cot who would hold the wet baby. Stories of monsters reappeared, and she asked to be rescued from the dark dungeon. In these frightening situations, she challenged me with the unspoken questions, "Is this a dangerous game? Will it be safe to go home?"

Loretta seemed to swing between hope and despair. She was proud her parents wanted her home and had worked so hard to keep her. She also had a new confidence in her capacities. At times, she enjoyed being the monster who frightened me, as well as the rescuer, for the feeling both of mastery and of revenge. Similarly, the gymnastic games were also about becoming skilful and brave, and Loretta could be watchful and careful of herself. She made attempts to mend some furniture in my room, as if to repair the damage of her previous angry onslaughts. Loretta showed me that it was the uncertainty that was so unbearable, not knowing if her parents' loving behaviour would turn to anger. I felt the same swings between optimism and doubt. I thought we were mirroring the family's volatile moods and their anxiety about facing the realities of their life together. I was relieved when I heard Loretta talking to a nurse about the butterflies in her tummy. It had now become more acceptable to admit her fears openly.

Her attempts to make sense of her abuse continued, accelerated by the prospect of her departure. She was much more aware of her capacity to think, once checking with me in a quiet moment if I "had a thought". I was aware how much she had progressed from the clinging child who could not acknowledge our separateness to her current state where she could observe me as her therapist and see what I had to offer her. She returned to the theme of "seeing and refusing to see" that often preoccupied her. Her anger about losing me put her in touch with her feelings about her abuse. She accused me of not caring, telling me not to look while she acted out a scene in which a mother hit her baby with a dirty nappy. The following session, she returned very distressed, throwing off her glasses, calling herself blind and stupid. She repeated the scene of the poisoning, the mother telling the child she hated her while she did it. Loretta's disillusion that I was allowing her to return to potential danger made her furious with herself for not foreseeing this. In the transference, I became at these moments like the mother who hated her and would therefore allow her to be attacked again.

Although Loretta had been open with me about her fears, she was very different in the community, protective of her mother, not wanting her upset. At times, her play about abuse appeared so real I felt anxious that it was being repeated. It soon became clear that the source of her current anxiety was renewed conflict between her parents. At the three-monthly review with the parents, they were confronted with the way they allowed Loretta to carry anxiety for the whole family and how they needed to take responsibility for their difficulties. We pointed out that, although Loretta had made progress in many areas, she was often regressed, clinging and insecure, unable to get on with her own development because she was so preoccupied with her concerns for her parents.

Her parents were able to respond to this with more appropriate parenting. Loretta regained her confidence, and I once again saw her become more outgoing in her play, imagining herself having adventures, going on journeys, making friends.

Loretta had been in treatment now for a year. At our last session before the Easter break, she was in touch with her fury and need, but she was able to use play to tell me how she felt she could not manage alone. She cut out a picture of me and then cut out my eyes and ears, throwing them in the bin, before throwing off her glasses. I talked about the way she threw away her ability to see and understand things if I was not around, but I stressed that she could think for herself. She grinned and retrieved a small piece, saying she would hold onto this, beginning to believe in her capacity to internalize our work.

Loretta was gradually integrated into a school in her local area. She was worried that she was damaged, unable to learn, comparing herself to a crashed car that had to be taken to the garage for mending. She regressed, wetting her pants, and told me how she wished she was still a baby; then she would not have to go to school and work so hard. After each of the early visits, Loretta came to her session full of pessimism. Once, she threw her glasses angrily against the wall, despite my attempts to stop her. We talked about how cross and worried she was about not managing in school. She recovered herself and went to the jigsaw puzzle, turning to this familiar game to calm herself, and she felt pleased when she fitted the pieces together. She was able to make sense of things again. By the end she was able to enjoy herself playing with the tractors, once more finding she had the latency skills she had felt were missing.

Despite her fears, Loretta did settle into the new school, saving her tiredness and difficult behaviour for when she came back to the Cassel.

Can things be mended? Preparing to go home

The last six months of treatment were dominated by Loretta's anxiety about her relationship with her parents and her fears about leaving. In her anger about ending treatment, Loretta parodied the idea of psychotherapy as a mending process, using the image of poison glue.

> Loretta introduced the idea of poison glue in a session in which she had begun in an angry mood throwing things around. She had not been well, and she was also on edge as she knew the family would soon be getting a leaving date. She noticed a crack in the wood of my desk and offered to mend it with Sellotape. Then she told me she had used "bad glue, poison". She told me that I had not looked after the table and that all my things were broken. I talked about her worry that things could not be mended and her fear that she might be poisoned if she goes home. She said, "No, Mum won't do it again".

When Loretta introduced the idea that her glue was poisoned, I felt shocked and tricked because I had thought that she was making amends for the mess she had made. I realized that, feeling abandoned, she was retaliating by mirroring her mother's abuse of her. Her apparent concern and wish to repair had become an attack on my room. At one level this was a triumphant reversal of roles, Loretta becoming an abuser rather than just a victim, but it was also a comment on her deeper distrust of relationships. She was showing me her fear that relationships can only be dangerous, that apparent care will turn out to be perverted. Afterwards she wanted the Sellotape to remain on the table to remind me of her, but this did not reassure her. She told me sadly: "Everything is broken."

This session highlighted the internal damage caused by the abuse. Loretta felt her own capacity to relate and care was easily turned to destructive poison by her anger and that others would treat her in a similar way. From her early life, Loretta had no internal model of a parental couple able to tolerate and work through destructive feelings, only of them being acted out in a concrete way. Over the months, this had changed, and the family were now able to share distress and anger more openly and safely, but the prospect of leaving made this progress seem very tenuous for Loretta. Sometimes she told me she would mend my room without bad glue, at other times she became frightened that there was poison glue on the floor and that I had put it there. This happened when she lost confidence after a hard day at school, or when the family discussed leaving and the reality seemed too frightening. The theme of babies being hurt returned, and there was always the question, "Who can be trusted?" Her fears once more got into me. She played out a scene of a child being locked in her bedroom, the mother becoming a monster, and I struggled to work out whether she was telling me something real or imagined.

At other times Loretta felt that she was being rushed, and she regressed into babyish behaviour, expecting me to do everything for her. When I protested, she said, "I can't clear up. I'll do it when I'm 7. I'm still hurt."

My summer holiday was the last long break in therapy before the family's departure, so it was an important preparation for ending. Loretta found it difficult while I was away, badly hurting her arm in a fall and becoming ill. Her parents also developed ailments. The family still used sickness as a way of drawing attention to their needs. When I returned, Loretta struggled to ward off feelings of sadness, saying she did not mind, but then had a furious tantrum. She brought soft toys to give her comfort, and she became more jealous of other children, realizing they would see me after she had gone. She pretended to lock me in my room so I could not see them. She also worried that these angry feelings would make me reject her, and she would try to make me feel good by pretending to make me tea.

Loretta continued to puzzle away at the issue of the abuse. Her new theory was that her mother had injured her because she had attacked mother's new baby, a reminder of the miscarriage and the jealous feelings this must have aroused. She also questioned her removal from home. Now in her play, it was a bad policeman who removed her, and a good one who took her back to her family. Remembering these times also made Loretta realize how vulnerable she had been as a baby. In one session, she sucked on a toy bottle, then said to me simply, "Mummy was not nice to me when I was a baby. I would not like to be a baby again."

As the weeks passed, Loretta counted down the sessions to leaving. The anxiety remained. She imagined a nice sunny home, feared it would become "disgusting", then reassured herself that her parents could look after her. She wondered, could she tell someone if something went wrong? She imagined calling the police, then worried anxiously that she would be punished if she did so. In the end she decided she would be safe. When she was anxious, she bumped and bruised herself often. Her mother became quite tearful about this, finding it hard to accept that Loretta still had worries. In her sessions, Loretta consoled herself by asking, "Who will I talk to? I'll talk to my hamster and my rabbit." She decided she would write me letters, and she copied my name off the name-plate on the door.

Three years on we hear that the family have settled back into the community and Loretta is doing well at school.

The impact of Munchhausen syndrome by proxy on emotional development

A central feature of Munchhausen syndrome by proxy is the lack of emotional containment in the family so that feelings of hatred and need are acted out on the body of a child. My work with Loretta suggests that the impact of living in a family with this pathology is to stultify many aspects of the child's emotional and cognitive development, as I describe below.

A protective skin

At the beginning of therapy, I was struck by Loretta's awkward, unkempt appearance and watchful look. As I got to know her, I could see how her physical awkwardness mirrored her emotional rigidity in which feelings were kept under tight control most of the time, except for occasional outbursts. I was reminded of Esther Bick's concept of a *second skin* (1968), a "muscular form of self containment" that a child constructs when there is insufficient emotional containment within the family to be introjected by the growing infant. It made me realize how dangerous it must feel to live in this family where a façade of competence covers despair and anger, covertly acted out in the injuries to the child. The child's awareness of her parents' ability to deceive other professionals and the secrecy habitual in these families would increase the sense of isolation and terror. The sense of unpredictability and feared loss of control in the parents would necessitate the owl-like vigilance Loretta described. As the child's therapist, I mirrored her continual state of anxiety, watchful of any changes in the child, fearful that the abuse was about to be repeated, never certain it would be safe to return home. It was the emotional containment offered by the hospital environment and my trust in the thinking and observing capacities of the other staff involved that made the process bearable and safe. Psychosocial nursing, psychotherapy, and the life of the hospital community all aimed to provide the same feeling of safety for the child.

Damage to the capacity to relate

Severe damage to the capacity to relate seems inevitable when basic trust and the need for reliable care have been violated. In this family, the child was caught up in an infantile clinging attachment to her mother, terrified to separate, yet fearful of closeness and her mother's hostility, the type of dangerous attachment she was describing in her image of *poison glue*. Loretta clearly sensed that, when her mother was in a state of fury or despair, there were no safe boundaries in her mother's mind between herself and her child and she was in danger of attack. Yet, at these times, she clung to her mother most fiercely. It was as if she and her mother were merged, and neither could bear to be separate and acknowledge the hatred in their relationship. The image of *poison glue* emerged in therapy only when Loretta knew that our relationship was ending. By this time, she was able to be more separate and reflective about her relationships, and so such clarity was possible. The suggestion of a dangerous attachment in the idea of poison glue communicates her experience of living in a perverse world as a vulnerable child, where intimacy is fraught with danger and the carer cannot be trusted. Her anxiety and fury about ending therapy evoked a similar mistrust in our therapeutic relationship that she felt was a mockery of treatment as she still felt damaged and frightened of the future. Her response was to retaliate and attack our relationship and then feel deeply sad about her destructiveness. What she described was a profound mistrust of herself and others that surfaced when she was disillusioned. Like the crack in the table in my room, this was an aspect of herself that she felt could not be mended. However, alongside this pessimism, there was always a longing for something different, a more nurturing and honest relationship. It is difficult to know whether this was innate in the child, or evidence of warmer moments in the early mother–infant relationship. Either way, it made it possible for me as a psychotherapist to establish a relationship with Loretta that helped her face what had happened and develop her potential.

Difficulties in separation and individuation

Difficulties in separation and individuation are central to this pattern of family functioning. There is so much insecurity within the family that a feeling of separateness and difference is intolerable. This lack of differentiation between parent and child in the parent's mind may contribute to the parent's use of the child's body to express distress or anger. The therapeutic task with each family member is to enable the process of individuation to begin. The child cannot achieve this without the support of the parent. At the beginning of therapy Loretta was so enmeshed with her parents that I could not tell what feelings were hers and what she carried for them. She became ill when the family were in conflict, somatizing their distress and hers, using her body in a way that mirrored the experience of the Munchhausen syndrome. As she gradually began to separate, I realized how she had used the powerful defences of denial and omnipotent control to protect herself from the feelings of disintegration and despair that surfaced when she faced her mother's murderousness. It took time before she could allow herself to explore these feelings, to question the hatred her mother felt towards her, and to recognize her own murderous wish to retaliate. Her increasing ability to make sense of events in her family, to fit the pieces together like the jigsaw in her play, seemed to relieve her of the confusion that was so disabling. As her therapist, I also began to find it easier to make sense of her sessions and see the progress that had occurred. The therapeutic relationship provided a space where the child could feel separate and observe the destructiveness in the family at a safe distance, with emotional support.

The parental couple

In this family the father was emotionally absent, rendered impotent in his child's mind by his failure to protect her from abuse. Later he was more able to fulfil his parental role, coming forward to care for Loretta when her mother was ill and acting as a buffer to reduce the intensity of their relationship. The capacity of the parents to begin to function with genuine concern was crucial to the child's progress. Loretta feared that she would be rejected if she became more separate and in touch with her feelings. It was the parents' grudging but real support for the therapy, encouraged by their own treatment, that gradually gave her confidence to begin to explore ideas and feelings.

Denial and cognitive delay

In families where life is based on denial and pretence, it is likely that the search for truth will be greatly resisted by a child and also longed for. As a result the child's capacity to think and understand is stultified. A recurrent image in Loretta's treatment was her use and abuse of her glasses to symbolize her ambivalence about using psychotherapy to see and understand the destructive and painful feelings within herself and her family. It was as if Loretta no longer dared think about what was happening to her. At times, she actively created confusion to make thinking impossible. This meant that she was unable to learn in school until she felt safe enough to begin using her mind in the more contained environment of hospital life and therapy. Loretta was clearly aware of her lack of cognitive development and ashamed of it, terrified that she was irreparably damaged. At the same time, she was so furious and frustrated about her condition that she tried to break her glasses to make any improvement impossible. Loretta had considerable capacities. What she had lacked was the experience of a thinking parent and the supportive environment necessary for these cognitive skills to develop.

Facing the depression and anger

In Munchhausen syndrome by proxy there is often the pretence of love and concern. In this family, I found little genuine expression of feeling. Denial and secrecy had become a habitual pattern, as it was too dangerous to express real emotions for fear of their destructiveness. The child, like the parents, usually related in a cold, detached way, and the expression of spontaneous warmth or loving feelings was rare. I felt we were beginning to make some progress when Loretta could express her experience of this emotional death in her images of dead or dying things. Once she began thinking and developing, her anger and depression surfaced. This was intolerable for her parents, who had tried to shut these feelings away. This made treatment very difficult, because their inability to confront Loretta's temper tantrums and her mother's retreat into silent fury and illness gave Loretta a feeling of frightening impotence. Their inability to set limits for Loretta made her more fearful of expressing herself. Ultimately, the parents did want their child to be helped, and this made it possible for them to tolerate gradually a greater expression of feeling, but for a long time during treatment the prospect of change felt very dangerous.

The need for emotional containment
for the family and workers

Treating a family who are so severely disturbed needs a secure and intensive inpatient setting with considerable support for staff and patients. In this family, the nature of relationships was very primitive, and they frequently became enmeshed in destructive conflict and withdrew into silence. Then it seemed that there were no boundaries—between parents and child, between their persecuted world and the reality of life in the community, between thought and action. At these times, the feeling of a lack of boundaries could pervade the treatment team, and it felt very unsafe to continue the work. We needed the containment provided by structures like nurse–therapy supervision and the unit and community staff meetings to process these feelings and to examine the family functioning in the wider context of the community. This made it possible to differentiate our anxiety and concerns from those of the family and to retain a sense of reality. Similarly, the hospital community and the treatment team provided clear boundaries for each individual and the family as a whole and made it safe for them to explore their frightening feelings without further acting out.

Work with the parents: understanding the abuse

Times of stress in this family gave us an indication of how the poisoning and other injuries occurred. It seems that the parents' hatred and despair with each other were projected onto the child and the child's body, which was attacked by the mother to eliminate these unbearable feelings. This became more understandable when we learned that both parents had been abused as children, and in attacking Loretta the mother was trying also to eradicate feelings of vulnerability and dependency. This left Loretta responsible for her parents' distress and well-being, and her behaviour became a barometer for the emotional state of the family. Work with the parents to enable them to separate and own their own feelings eventually made it possible for Loretta to have a sense of herself as an individual with some control and competence in her life.

As the diagnosis of Munchhausen syndrome by proxy suggests, Loretta's illnesses and injuries had been used by the parents, particularly the mother, to get attention for their own distress. During treatment, the focus moved onto her own body, and her many requests for physical investigations were an opportunity to look at the meaning of her somatization. This freed Loretta of the burden of being the sick one, although it was a difficult role to give up, and she continued to get herself bruised and injured if she was worried about the family. What became clear in our work with the family was that the poisonous feelings belonged to the parents' relationship. If they could be helped to face their fury with each other that each could not meet the other's great feelings of deprivation, then Loretta could be released from carrying these feelings and could take on the role of the child who needs care and nurturing. The family gradually became more able to do this, setting firm boundaries and responding to Loretta's distress and anger with sincere concern.

The development of a new internal model

The aspect of the abuse that Loretta had found hardest to face was that her mother had hated her enough to wish to kill her, and at times Loretta could not believe she could ever be a loveable child. The fact that this rehabilitation went ahead gave her parents an opportunity to repair the damage and to offer a different model of themselves as concerned parents and herself as a loved child, which Loretta could internalize and use as a model for herself.

As the therapy progressed, I could see crucial signs of change in Loretta—her moves towards independence and learning, the beginning of warmth and concern, and a more ordinary attachment to her parents replacing the anxious clinging. As her father and maternal grandparents became more central figures in Loretta's life, she felt more protected by the family network and less caught up in an exclusive relationship with her mother. I hoped that the internal changes Loretta achieved in therapy would be sustained by a more positive experience of family life in the future.

CHAPTER FOUR

Psychoanalytic aspects of inpatient treatment of abused children

Denis Flynn

his chapter looks at the experience of inpatient hospital treatment at the Cassel Hospital and how formal psychoanalytic psychotherapy, with its emphasis on the transference and the inner world, fits into that context and orientates itself to some of the realities of the setting. It outlines how psychotherapy and psychosocial nursing can work to inform and enrich each other, and what is psychoanalytic about the overall work. A bridge of understanding is built using the patients' perceptions of, adjustment to, and conflict about the inpatient setting, and the affective impact of the processes on patients and staff alike. Two clinical examples of severe child-abuse family cases are given, the first of Munchhausen syndrome by proxy, the second in which a baby sibling had been killed. They show how in-depth psychoanalytic work with mother and child and individual psychotherapy of the child can be combined with psychotherapy of the parents and intensive work in the therapeutic community. Such a combination can contribute, even in cases of severe pathology, to the development of the relationship between mother and child and promote successful rehabilitation in the outside community.

The setting

Treatment of the severely disturbed patient in an inpatient setting provides particular opportunities for supportive containment of the patient as well as particular dangers of severe regression and intensified disturbance. How inpatient treatment works, and whether and why it works depend on how different aspects of treatment are brought together. What is on offer in inpatient treatment at the Cassel Hospital is not just psychoanalytic under-standing and insight in individual and group psychotherapy, together with intensive psychosocial nursing in a therapeutic com-munity context, but a range of types of care. These include some tangible benefits, such as food, an overnight bed, spare time, and opportunities for pleasures including recreational time and activi-ties. They also include the company of other patients in a shared communal living and treatment space. There are also other aspects of inpatient treatment apart from what is specifically psychoana-lytic. Among the most important are real bodily care; levels of protection, from total exposure to the real pressures of outside life, and, within the hospital itself, from harmful and abusive attacks by others; real sanctions to be invoked to prevent or reduce self-abusive attacks; and supervision and appraisal of child-care issues and individual psychiatric mental state, as appropriate. I should like to discuss in this chapter how a key area of the overall treatment—namely, the area of nurse–psychotherapist coopera-tion—evolves and how the treatment is, despite the complexities of the setting, truly psychoanalytic.

Traditionally, psychoanalytic psychotherapy can take place only when the patient's ego is strong enough, and the level of motivation sufficient, for him or her to accept the limitations of the psychoanalytic settings, to attend the same place at agreed times, and to accept rules of abstinence from actual libidinal relation-ships with the therapist and rules of restraint from aggressive attacks upon the therapist. For the borderline patient who has failed in treatment elsewhere, who may be caught in a chronic cycle of suicidal or self-abusive attacks, or for the abusing parent who primarily wants the child returned home from foster care, such preconditions are rarely there from the outset. Indeed, tradi-tional criteria of analysability may possibly be there at the end of treatment, but rarely before. Zetzel (1970) lists these criteria as follows: the capacity to tolerate love and hate of the same object, to distinguish external and internal reality, to experience relationships on a genital level, to tolerate expressions of affect, to be capable of sustaining emotional growth, to be able to deal with underlying hostility and aggression, and to be able to internalize and identify on the basis of a new relationship.

The organization of inpatient treatment

Psychoanalytic treatment is possible at the Cassel because the patient is held in treatment by the mutually cooperative effort of nurse and therapist, and by the sustained involvement of patients and staff together in a "culture of enquiry" within the therapeutic community. There are many areas of shared aims and focus, particularly in concentrating attention on the capacity of the patient actively to address his or her problems around what Kennedy (1987) has called the "work of the day" of everyday life that gives a structure to the patient managing the day.

Within the therapeutic-community context of the hospital, patients have responsibility for their own treatment, and parents have an actual and real responsibility for their children throughout the day and night (Flynn, 1987, 1988). Nurses working alongside will help to make emotional sense of what the patients are doing, dealing not just with eruptions of disturbed behaviour, but with the patients' capacities to take on specific responsibilities and tasks.

The day is organized so that there is only one meal—lunch prepared by hospital staff—which gives time for patients to have therapeutic meetings with nurses, activities, and psychotherapy sessions. The other meals are organized and prepared by patients. There is practical work to be done: cleaning, cooking, ordering food and planning menus, and managing the therapeutic budgets. There are the ordinary tasks of the family with children: getting dressed, preparing for school in the Children's Centre, having breakfast, and, after school, finding appropriate leisure activities, evening meals, baths for children, settling down, managing the night-time. In unit or "firm" meetings, emotional issues are discussed.

There are three units: family, adolescent, adult. All patients from these units come together in community meetings to discuss emotional issues affecting the whole community. Some patients become "firm chair" or "community chair", each for three months or so, and are actively involved with the other patients during the day and in evening structures, such as the night meeting. From 7 p.m. until 8 a.m. there are only one nurse and a night orderly in the hospital, with duty-team back-up, so patients effectively manage their emotional issues together. It is the task of the "firm chair" and "community chair", and all the patients, to hear and respond to concerns in the "night meeting", to respond directly, aid the nurse with crises, and bring pressing and relevant issues into the more formally structured day meetings. Staff review individuals' progress and the community and firm process in daily staff meetings, and other formal meetings, which involve nurses and psychotherapists together. In a weekly "strains" meeting, attended by all the clinical staff, the emotional impact of the work on the staff is examined, including current pressures and strains between staff. In effect, this looks at the countertransference processes in the staff working with these patients in a therapeutic community setting.

The role of nurse and psychotherapist

There are essential differences between nursing and therapy, and each brings something quite distinct to treatment. Potentially there is the possibility of conflict between them, but also of something creative and new. There is a long tradition of psychoanalytically informed nursing at the Cassel, especially in the way nurses use their own experience of patients as a central guide to their understanding of them individually and in community and institutional processes (Barnes, 1968; Griffiths & Pringle, 1997; Kennedy, 1986). At a deeper level, the therapist and nurse are at best like a couple whose sexuality is complementary, who, starting with separate capacities, can think and work together, can sustain some conflict and yet offer something essential and distinctive together.

While each will focus on the current processes of the patient's treatment over the previous twenty-four hours, nurse and therapist have separate tasks and separate roles. The therapist concentrates primarily on an understanding of the patient as it becomes apparent in the individual transference. The nurse primarily seeks to elucidate the nature of the patient's capacities as manifested in daily activities and relationships, guiding the patient with plans and strategies for moving forward, keeping in the forefront the emotional meaning, quality, and impact of his or her behaviour and plans of action. Particular attention is paid to developing the active capacities of patients, yet often challenging entrenched habits and defences, using ordinary human reactions and responses. Each nurse and therapist will be aware of the work of the other and will integrate an awareness and understanding of the work of the other into their contact with the patient. This does not mean that the nurse makes psychoanalytic interpretations; rather, his or her contact with the patient is informed by psychoanalytic insights. Similarly, the therapist's understanding does not come simply from his or her knowledge of the patient in the consulting-room; rather, she or he will be aware how the patient is functioning within the therapeutic community, within the family, and in the relationship between patient and nurse. This provides valuable information to set alongside what is emerging in the individual transference and may lead to an understanding of wider transferences, including split transferences—for example, to the nurse or to the hospital, or parts of it.

Each worker within the therapeutic community will have some knowledge of the work of others, including some knowledge of the current psychodynamic issues for patients and staff and, indeed, some sense of one's role within the institution. Equally, both nurse and therapist know something of the work of the other. For example, the therapist would know of the nurse's focus and the state of the patient's response to the care plan, while the nurse knows that certain painful and intimate details of the patient's life are being taken up in the individual psychotherapy or, alternatively, that there is a period of sterile resistance. But when either nurse or therapist becomes too identified with the task of the other, without keeping to his or her own focus and perspective, something may be going wrong in the treatment. In a comparable way, if the individual patient, or the patient group, sees the hospital or the staff lumped together—for example, as "useless" or "all bad"—they can be perceived as the "combined object" of the parents, in Melanie Klein's terms, where the good and bad aspects of nurse and therapist and aspects of therapeutic community life cannot be differentiated and separately experienced. As Tom Main outlined in "The Ailment" (1957), the strain of working in what becomes a hostile environment can manifest itself in a decline in the health and capacities of the staff. It is in just such cases of primitive attacks that the staff themselves can begin to lose their own identity and capacity to work in their separate ways, and their effective functioning together may disintegrate. This can lead to breakdown and failure in individual cases, to individual break-down of staff members, to effective splitting of the staff team, and to the possibility of retaliatory attacks by the staff upon the patients, or vice versa.

The psychoanalytic aspects of psychosocial nursing

Psychosocial nursing is different in kind from psychotherapy in its quality and depth of awareness and in its focus on promoting adolescent and adult development, but it is, I believe, also psychoanalytic. Much of the essential work of the nurse is to increase the capacity of patients to relate and to help patients learn to distance themselves from all-consuming aspects of personal conflict that take them away from a focus or direction in life and can reduce the ordinary to the superficial or the irrelevant. Nursing aims to relate, to engage, to confront, to reduce superficiality, to restore purpose. As such, it is essential to the work with the underlying narcissistic base of the patient's problems. Patients have to face wider concerns, not just the near horizons of their own pathology.

For patients and staff alike, such work has a life-restoring function, bringing new interest and purpose. It can move the patient out of the quagmire of regressions and regressive distortions towards something more alive and normal. Work is done with each patient and the community as a whole to see the effects of actions, for better or worse, on others. There certainly can be an emotional strain from the unremitting quality of the work at times. However, staff may be prepared to work long-term in a place where ongoing difficult and painstaking work with the destructive fragments and depressed sides of the patients may lead, with some relief, to a recurrent process where steps are taken towards something more lively and restored. Effective working together of therapist and nurse can have a supportive and restorative effect for both of them and can produce more ongoing cooperative effort in the work.

Clarification of a theoretical difference

Opinions concerning which elements of the inpatient treatment process are "mutative"—that is, produce lasting psychic change—have varied over time, depending on how the process is conceptualized. I think opinion has swung from thinking that mutative change occurs by a deep working through in individual therapy of central features of the underlying pathology to a view that important change occurs through sustained nursing work within the therapeutic community. In an influential paper, Muir (1986) has argued that, because patients come to the Cassel following severe breakdowns in normal functioning and capacities, the psychotherapy should combine forces with nursing to improve functioning. My view, as stated earlier, is that there is not just one process, nor one unified technique, but different aspects of treatment. Patients form transferences to both nurse and therapist, and to other important figures and indeed to aspects of the hospital, depending on the level of their affective contact—that is, feeling towards and depth of relationship with each. Nurses also draw the transference around ordinary household issues to themselves, as they work alongside the patients in the kitchen, the pantry, activities groups, and they can, more quickly than therapists, become the focus of a community or institutional transference

(Barnes, 1968; Barnes et al., 1997; Flynn, 1987; Griffiths & Pringle, 1997). However, something essential is lost in terms of understanding inpatient work if classical psychoanalytic aspects of the transference to the individual psychotherapist in the clinical session are dispensed with, since this is an essential part of the ongoing process of understanding the patient's world.

Some aspects of the transference may be apparent early on, but the patient's transference to the therapist and to the hospital becomes apparent only as time goes on. The patient's ways of relating—what is true behaviour and what reflects his or her true internal state—are by no means immediately obvious. What is true is not simply something discovered or uncovered, but something we recognize when we have arrived at it, and then we find we need to treat what we may have thought of as peripheral or unimportant as more serious or, indeed, as the central issue (Bion, 1962a). This arrival at the truth may come from psychotherapy or nursing, or, interestingly, from both at once, after the importance of what we each have been struggling with has been fully recognized.

I think there is a confusion about this rooted in James' original paper (1984) on nurse–therapist supervision, where, as with Muir and others referred to above, there is the assumption that there is a shared task between nurse and therapist. James divides therapeutic behaviours between nurse and therapist as if they cooperatively plan to divide up the therapeutic task. According to James, the therapist will elucidate, the nurse confront: "Generally, nurses do more registering of a patient's distorted or inappropriate relating, and therapists do more relating. ... The therapist does not draw attention to inappropriate behaviour ... as it is happening ... the nurse does so frequently." A stated consequence of this view is that it is only the nurse who is seen to have adequate "affective contact" with the patient or patients. James argues that the principal task of nurse–therapist supervision is to enable the therapist to intervene in the relationship between nurse and patient. In my view, therapeutic behaviours of nurse and therapist are not so prescribed, and indeed it is the therapist who will often confront the patient to bring out in the session the reality of the patient's interactions in their family and the therapeutic community, and the nurse's work will often elucidate in a graphic and meaningful way the inner world of the patient. I shall show this in my two clinical examples below.

Nurse–therapist supervision

Both nurse and therapist, then, will have affective contact with the patient and what is most useful in nurse–therapist supervision is to understand the differences of therapeutic approach and the conflicts that come to light. Nurse–therapist supervisions are different and additional to other supervisions of clinical work. A senior therapist and a senior nurse meet with a primary team of workers with a family, including the nurse, the child psychotherapist, and the adult psychotherapist. One or other of the workers will elect to speak first, talking of how they find working with the family, how they are working in their role, and how they are communicating or not with the other workers. Each of the workers will follow; then the supervisors will pick out themes. It is important not to make it into a formal review and to keep it to a degree experiential, so that one may feel and see that there may be processes of re-enactment at work in relation to each other or one or both of the supervisors: for example, is one of the workers feeling squeezed out, dropped, neglected, and murderous towards the rival? This work requires a degree of freedom and trust of each other, to be able to bring out in a group of workers countertransference feelings that may show up how adequately one is working in one's role with the family and how able one is to work with other professionals and, in many cases, for therapists and nurses to make use of their own experience of personal psychoanalysis. In general I believe that the nurse–therapist supervision is experienced by staff as invaluable in developing working alliances when working with families that have intense disturbance and where there may be hidden, severely destructive splitting processes. Some consideration can be given to how the nurse–therapist supervision that was developed at the Cassel may be adaptable to other settings (Bandler, 1987).

Clinical examples

Case one

In my first clinical example, I illustrate how a psychoanalytic understanding takes shape in this particular type of inpatient setting. Three points are emphasized:

1.   supervision of disturbed or abusing patients;
2.   work with underlying destructiveness;
3.   problems of intense dependence.

This is an important area of applied psychoanalytic work which we have been doing on the Families Unit for over a decade—that is, the rehabilitation of severely abused children or their siblings. I shall restrict my focus and briefly illustrate how work from one arena (nursing), combined with awareness of processes of treatment as a whole, help develop the work in another arena (child psychotherapy), and vice versa. The case is one of Munchhausen syndrome by proxy (see chapter two; see also Kennedy & Coombe, 1995) where two children had nearly been killed through systematic poisoning by salt, for which the mother eventually accepted responsibility. The poisoning had occurred in a clandestine and murderous fashion over a period of many months. The two children who had been poisoned had now gone to an alternative placement, and the mother, Ms Smith, and new baby, Jane, were currently in treatment, after being under twenty-four-hour surveillance in a mother–baby psychiatric unit for the first eleven months.

The view of the adult psychotherapist who saw Ms Smith for individual psychotherapy (twice weekly), and later for group psychotherapy, was that her central psychopathology involved an incapacity to bear separation or difference. This underwent some degree of modification through the Cassel experience. She characteristically avoided experience of loss by various means, including denial, reaction formation, manic flight, and hostile devaluing of the object. She had a harsh and envious element that could become obscured, warded off, or controlled under many circumstances. It was clear that there was a psychotic centre to her personality, and there had been one previous psychotic breakdown, which oc-curred when she was briefly separated from her new baby after an emergency protection order.

Mother–infant sessions

Mother–infant sessions take place weekly in the Families Unit when working with severe child abuse cases and involve a child psychotherapist and sometimes a nurse. They are set up so that the mother can discuss with the child psychotherapist any issues of concern about the infant. The child psychotherapist can observe and work with the here-and-now of the mother–infant relation-ship, integrating outside observations from within the hospital or the foster home. When there is a father or stepfather involved, they sometimes also attend. Most of the infants are returning to their mothers after being in foster care. A few toys are provided, and the mother is encouraged to bring some of the child's own toys. The sessions are usually very emotionally charged, and in most cases there are contentious legal issues about whether mother and infant should be together. Often, after abuse and neglect, and having lost and indeed missed out on emotional contact with the child, the mothers need to recognize and face up to aspects of their way of relating to the child that are hindering a deepening of their bond. Mothers need to be able to accept respon-sibility for what happened and, as treatment goes on, further blame, shame and painful awareness, so the sessions work against the danger of contact with the child being lost and weak links severed. This is especially so if the mother cannot accept responsi-bility. In effect, the mother does not bond again with the infant unless she can get beyond the abusive behaviour or her part in the abusive experience. If, as often happens, a defensive or protective shell is created around the mother–infant couple, the habitual responses of mother to child may be ignored, along with the infant's attempts at communication and his or her changing devel-opmental needs.

When I began in the mother–infant sessions in this case, the quality of Ms Smith's conversation about Jane was inconsequential "coffee-morning talk" about the child's development and interest in food, toys, and people, delivered in a monotonous nasal drone. It was hard to get to specific emotional truths about what was going on. Ms Smith was very stuck in her bizarre, unreal accounts, which were full of denial. Nevertheless, at some level I felt there was a genuine attachment to Jane, and some hope of change. Jane herself was not very appealing and had a way of throwing her head back and making a groaning guttural shout, which sounded distressing and disconnected. She did not experience her mother as being able to cope with her discomfort and distress, and she hid her hurt when she got a knock or seemed to hide her needs if she wanted something. Her mother generally did not notice.

The atmosphere in treatment was a difficult one. Ms Smith's own mistrust of others was projected into people around her, so she then had to protect herself from them with an "armour" of deviousness and pseudo-normality. She resented bitterly the supervision that was organized to keep the child safe and, as with many patients in this category, put much of her energy into thwarting the efforts of the nursing and therapy staff. She felt watched in the hospital and that I was watching her and Jane in sessions, which made her more false and compliant. Work with this meant that a crucial link was made between a major conflict for Ms Smith in the hospital, in a wider transference, and what was then going on in the here-and-now transference of the mother–infant session. I took up her fear of being watched by me, while relating it to what was happening more widely. The result was that I saw a more fluid contact from mother to infant than I had seen so far and the possibility of something more real and flexible between them. Interpreting Ms Smith's responses to supervision then, and linking them to issues of the lack of contact between mother and child, brought out transference issues in relation to the whole treatment. Following this work, she was able to acknowledge the tension of being observed and her wish to isolate herself and cut herself off.

A lot of the nursing work at the Cassel involves working in groups: morning work groups, group meetings, group recreational activities. Ms Smith liked to work on her own or with one other person whom she would control. At first she managed to get into solitary work groups, like the laundry work group, and became manager of the sewing activity, and then gardening manager, each time working hard but on her own. Her nurse then worked to steer her towards contact with other patients. Her wish to cut herself off or dominate made the therapy groups, which were introduced during her stay, particularly hard to bear (see chapter two).

In the ensuing months the problems had to get considerably worse before they got better. We were then seeing more of the underlying destructiveness. Her two older children were at this stage going to a permanent placement, and her relationship with her own parents had now broken down. Ms Smith's way of coping with these real losses of her mother, stepfather, husband, and children was to replace them with a search for her real father. This inability to deal with losses is important aetiologically, especially the inability to mourn her maternal grandmother, who died just before the birth of her first child (whom she poisoned), and the loss of her natural father as a child, which had contributed to the embittered relationship with her mother throughout childhood. It was important for her nurse, and the adult and child psychothera-pists, to work continuously with her holidays and absences. Her nurse also helped her to say goodbye to the children she had previously poisoned. They met with the father and social worker, and the mother spent an hour with them explaining that she wanted them to live with daddy and that she was sorry but she was not able to keep them safe. She gave them a photograph album with pictures of their childhood. This was a moving good-bye, and, after being very upset, she told her nurse that this was the first time she had felt that these were her two children.

The issue of loss became more acute when a foster home was found where Jane could go at the weekends. This was arranged to facilitate a degree of separateness between mother and child and to allow Ms Smith space in her flat at weekends on her own away from the intensity of the treatment. To Ms Smith this signified the unpalatable fact that Jane could be a separate person; it also underlined the fact that rehabilitation might not work out, which created a feeling in her of not being totally in control and brought intense conflict for her. The level of Ms Smith's paranoia about other people increased. Just prior to a difficult case conference, she caused severe injury to her own hands. Her anger was directed against the staff, in particular her nurse, who suffered a sustained and unmitigated barrage of attacks. Later her anger came out with

Jane. An incident occurred within the hospital in which the child
was put into an over-hot (though not scalding) bath. This was
taken very seriously by all concerned. Paradoxically, however,
when the hidden murderousness began to surface and Ms Smith
had to acknowledge it, she became more workable.

We now began to see more of the range and depth of her
destructiveness, and some of the psychodynamic patterns. Ms
Smith was excessively controlling, so that Jane's independent
development and play was hindered in various ways. Jane had
begun to develop several traits just like her mother, some areas of
competence such as speech, and some unhealthy behaviour, such
as bullying other children. In response to this continuous interference by her mother, bodily and psychosomatic elements appeared, such as a lengthy period of chest infections and some
asthma. During the hospital tests for this, Ms Smith accused others
of putting poisonous substances into the child. Her nurse saw that
Jane had been on six courses of antibiotics in a period of eight
weeks. She was very concerned that Ms Smith might be doing
something to cause these illnesses. When she asked Ms Smith
outright if she was doing anything to Jane, Ms Smith was furious
with her nurse. This was a very useful piece of work, Ms Smith
being faced with the reality both of what she was doing now and
the reality that she had poisoned her two children. Another focus
of the nurse's work was to help Ms Smith voice ambivalent
feelings she had about Jane. When Jane had chickenpox and was
in semi-isolation on the family unit landing, Ms Smith was able to
say how trapped she felt and how difficult she found it being with
her daughter all the time. Ms Smith could voice her feelings and
her complaint, and her nurse could hear it. The other patients
could take her complaint as normal, and people responded to her
needs by offering to baby-sit to give her a break. This was so
important, because, before the poisoning of her children, Ms
Smith had, like many other perpetrators in Munchhausen syndrome by proxy cases, repeatedly visited her GP asking for help,
but none was given, and the precipitate danger not registered.

After several more months of painstaking work with mother
and child, there were some signs of change in the child. She was
happier and more relaxed and began relating directly to me on
occasions. I have found in mother–infant sessions that the capacity

of the child to have a separate relationship with the child psycho-therapist is a good prognostic sign. This usually is indicative of some increase in security and some ego development in the child. It can show that the child feels that her mother is able to make contact with the child psychotherapist, so she has permission to do so too. In this case it meant that the work could go deeper to underlying issues about dependence and desperation. It became possible at last to look at Ms Smith's now voiced near-psychotic fear that, if she allowed Jane to change, she would grow into an "alien child". Underneath this was the terrifying fear that she would personally reject Jane as she had the others, with terrifying consequences if her actions went out of control. Jane's own anxie-ties about separation from the symbiotic level of closeness with her mother now began to come out. When actual separations occurred, Jane began to wake at night in the hospital screaming. She reacted adversely to any strange situation, which she seemed to take in an unprocessed way and which then seemed to haunt her. Both the mother and child had to cope with intense anxiety during separations. The mother–infant sessions aimed to help them understand this and adjust to changing ways of relating.

Since discharge and successful rehabilitation into the outside community, the family and the outside workers have had follow-up consultations over the last few years. The ongoing assessments are encouraging and there have been no causes for alarm that the child would be harmed. Ms Smith is very successful in her area of work, and Jane now has a number of friends and is getting on well at school. Although the work was successful at one level, we are aware that much more could have been done if this patient had been able to accept further intensive psychotherapy that had been offered in a specialist outpatient setting, and recent consultations show that severe splitting processes and glimpses of the underly-ing murderousness become apparent from time to time.

Case two

In my second clinical example, I look at how a psychoanalytic understanding of a mother and child, separately and together, took shape in my work relating to the work of the nurse and the whole hospital treatment. It is inevitably an abbreviated account, and I shall concentrate on the child's experience.

This is a family in which a 4-week-old baby, Helen, had been killed by horrific non-accidental injuries, with neglect and injury from the age of 1 week. The mother, Susan, and an older child, Ann, were being rehabilitated after the mother came out of prison. The baby's father, Ann's stepfather, had been convicted of the injuries and the killing and was still in prison. Ann was now 2 years 9 months old: she had been 1 year 3 months when the baby was killed. Ann had been plucked into care immediately in an emergency way, without any preparation or goodbyes, and had remained in a foster home. Along with the range of other therapy and nursing work, mother–infant work looked at whether the mother could rebond with her child. Later, in parallel individual psychotherapy from the age of 3 years, Ann was helped to face the break up of the family, the broken bond with her mother, and the trauma of the killing, which she had probably witnessed (Black et al., 1993).

While in prison Susan had had eight months of once-weekly psychotherapy. Her prison therapist thought of her as having a dangerous capacity for denial. This period of psychotherapy proved, however, to be an important preparation for the subsequent attempts at rehabilitation, especially in bringing some recognition of the extent of her own state of disturbance and her own wish to be reunited with her child to try to become a mother again.

In Susan's therapy, in the mother–infant sessions, and in their work with nurses—and, indeed, with patients in the community— prominent features from the start were evidence of trauma, flashbacks, and nightmares in mother and child, a marked trait in the mother of ambivalent and oscillating attachments, and persistent deviousness in her behaviour, particularly in relation to professionals. Although mother and child had some wish to be together, at first there was no real bond between them. Susan was sometimes cold and cruel to Ann and thoughtless about her needs. There was also in Susan an inner guilt and a wish to be punished, and so to lose her child. Awareness of this guilt led to further cycles of projections. The Cassel was then seen, not as the prison, as it had been seen, but as the hideously depriving and longed-for mother. Susan could act in quite a schizoid way, when her capabilities and functioning disintegrated. Ann learnt to develop a pseudo-closeness to her mother to deal with the painful experience of her dissociated states.

The family nurse found that, when Susan was in these states of mind, Ann became more distressed, her sleeping pattern became disturbed, she was more clingy, and she asked for her dummy continuously. Susan found these times even more traumatizing when she realized her effect on Ann. She swung from thinking, "No, I can't look after Ann" to "Yes, I must", with great rapidity, and with a dispersal of the previously felt immobilizing anxiety that was alarming in itself. It was a reminder of her capacity to deny, to split her mental states and cut herself off from the reality of her difficulties, which her nurse was helping her to face. Threatened by these sudden changes, Ann was often very angry with her mother, biting and pinching her. This brought out how guilty and bad Ann felt. It proved immensely difficult for her nurse to help them with the painfulness of their relationship. This was particularly so since Ann could not tolerate her mother being with a third person. Her nurse found that, when she got involved, Ann desperately tried to oust her, saying, "Go away", or pretending to fall asleep or demanding attention. Ann looked intensely to her mother for her needs and cuddles, and imitated her, wearing her clothes and shoes and mimicking her smoking manner and ways of talking to people, in an attempt to keep her mother by a primitive identification.

Within a short time, Susan encountered considerable difficulties accepting the supervision arrangements within the hospital, and it became apparent that she felt unsafe. Susan, however, could honestly see this, and after a fortnight she requested a temporary separation, when Ann went back to foster-parents for a week. This initial realism and acceptance of the depth of her problem—that she might not manage to have the child back—though disruptive for Ann, meant that we could look at the reality of the difficulties. On Ann's return to the hospital, the effects of the disruption were indeed apparent.

In the next mother–infant session a couple of days later, Ann looked very tired and flustered and Susan was again in a bored and disconnected state. There was little contact or communication between them, and Ann was left to her own devices and wandered around the room aimlessly. The painful experience with mother was dissociated; she ignored her mother's punitiveness to her and said to me instead, "I'm not talking to you." I then became for her the rejected and rejecting transference figure.

The early transference of the mother to the child psychotherapist formed part of a process of splitting of the "good motherly man" as distinct from the "bad/fascinating man" (Welldon, 1992). Usually I was seen as the former. But of particular concern was a relationship that the mother had with a man in the hospital who had been and could be violent, and the possibility that there could be a repetition of how the family violence had occurred.

In one session Ann took one of the Duplo men figures and put it in a chair in the dolls' house watching the television. It fell out, and I asked her if she wanted me to put it back in one of the chairs. She said, "No", and insisted that I put it in the particular seat where she consistently put it, the one where the man sits and watches the television. I felt that she was aware of me as someone watching and listening regularly and being consistent in that position. I interpreted that it was important for Ann that I could be the man to sit and watch and to help her think about being back with her mother.

From the nurse in the playgroup I now learnt that Ann was becoming preoccupied with babies, how to bath them, put them asleep, and so on. She brought a huge baby-size doll to the mother–infant sessions. It was clear that this related to her awakening preoccupations with how babies were treated and what had happened to the baby in her family.

After four months, however, a serious problem developed in the mother–infant sessions; the mother was preventing the child from having more open contact with me, limiting the effectiveness of my contact with her. A change in structure was therefore needed, so that there would be one individual psychotherapy session per week, with one mother–infant session per week to run in parallel. This change of structure came sooner than usual. I would usually move directly from mother–infant sessions to individual sessions when the child had developed a capacity to relate to me separately, the need for the joint sessions was passed, and the whole process worked through with the mother and child. This time I was pressured by the courts outside to see if the mother could not just keep the child safe but allow her to be separate and express what she felt. This in turn put a pressure on me and, indeed, on the child to adjust very quickly to what was happening. I think that this pressure reflected not just a difficult technical issue, or a particular difficulty in an applied setting, but reflected something for the child and indeed her mother—namely, how a change of outlook and a deep internal change was necessary and how thinking and feelings had to be processed rapidly in a very complete way if mother and child were to be rehabilitated together.

In her first individual session, Ann began with a game of toy trains. Then she repeatedly dropped toy animals from her head onto the floor. She spoke of mummy and daddy while playing with the small figures from the family set. I mentioned to her that she had seen daddy (at the prison) yesterday. She smiled and laughed, saying she was given sweeties, and seemed pleased. When one of the animals fell off her head, a gorilla figure, she said it was "killed", though it was not clear by whom. She now placed a woman figure in the chair looking at the television, whereas in previous play it had been a man. The woman was then bathed and put on the toilet. Ann then became preoccupied about how the plugs and the taps worked. She involved me in a game with her of making them work. She did traces of my hand on the paper, and she wrote lists of children's names. She finally also pointed out to me that one of the chairs was mended.

My impression as the session went on was that Ann felt more contained because she was being thought about and understood on her own, and she now could make more sense of what she felt and saw (Bion, 1962a). Overall, I had the impression that Ann was beginning to talk about things that could be broken, that could fall away, perhaps be hurt by falling. She mentioned "killing", but evident too was a sense of things being mended and repaired. She was perhaps only working from "traces", as she traced the shape of my hand and hers, and she was concerned with naming new relationships and ordering her new knowledge, by means of the list of children's names.

In the following joint session, the mother told me a dream that Ann had told her which had scared her. She had woken up saying there was "a fat man on the ceiling", and she had shown fear, even terror, talking about it. It sounded to me as if it was a dream that was so realistic that Ann had repeated it as if it were still going on after she had woken. Now, as mother spoke to me, Ann listened and then said, "There is a fat man on the ceiling." She soon reverted to her regressed use of the dummy and said she was not talking to me. This time I felt that the not talking to me was a way of protecting her mother from the things she might say. At the same time she ran the bottom of her shoes up her mother's leg, taunting her, getting under her skin, mirroring how her mother taunted her sometimes. I thought that this taunting was a veiled way of indicating that she knew about more serious forms of hurting and being hurt, to do with her painful memories of separation from her mother and possibly with memories about the baby. Susan herself could fearfully accept a possible understanding of the dream that "the fat man on the ceiling" might refer to a composite memory of a man and a baby, a sort of screen memory of the child lying in her cot and being preoccupied with the baby. It was an important part of the work with the mother, and she could bear to learn something of what Ann had gone through, would now know more about it, and would have to adjust to it emotionally. Sometimes she could bear it, but at other times she again produced more erratic and schizoid behaviour.

Despite some periods of listlessness and despair, and other periods of manic dissociated identification with her mother's more disturbed behaviour, Ann was developing a strength in itself. What she needed to be allowed to know and express had an urgency that went beyond her mother's disruptive behaviour and incapacity to digest what was happening emotionally for her and Ann. It was striking that, as Ann's work on mourning for her sister and the loss of her mother (and stepfather) developed, and when she felt overall more settled with her mother, her nurse could do the overdue work around potty training. Her nurse had been very aware of how Ann would regularly "shut down" her capacity for awareness, such as at the weekends when she went back to the foster-parents, going into a mindless forgetful state. Such behaviour had been very puzzling and painful. It seemed that Ann's anxiety was that she was required to hold in her anger, her feelings and needs, and indeed deaden herself, in an unconscious way doing what she felt was demanded of her, in identification with the dead baby. Now, after some time, Ann could "let go" in different ways, and the potty training was achieved very quickly, so that her contact with her mother was strengthened.

In another individual session Ann now played out a scene, explaining everything to me as she did it, where the man smashes an armchair and is very naughty for doing it. She threw the chair vigorously and shouted loudly. Ann spoke clearly and with possession and pride about "her times", as if increasingly realizing her need for some privacy in her containment of her inner experience. But there were other signs of distress, such as her deliberate nose-poking, which caused regular bleeding. When this was talked about in a mother–child session, Ann went to pieces and started asking in a monotone for "dummy-mummy". She seemed to make use of her mother's own defensive attitudes, and sometimes she hid behind a mother who did not or would not understand and would keep anxiety away, "the dummy-mummy". Later on, she continued her explorations. She took a toy Duplo diver and wrapped the string from its helmet round her leg and spoke of her leg being broken. She laughed and was then able to take the dummy out of her mouth. Ann was currently becoming upset about babies again, especially one who was leaving the hospital prematurely and without warning as rehabilitation broke down. Susan sat thinking reflectively about how Ann stroked this baby in the same way she used to stroke the baby that was killed.

Ann's anger with her mother and stepfather was emerging much more now, in various ways. She would usually quickly deny her anger and anxiously tell her mother she loved her, making an open show of rejecting me instead. The mother would flaunt this in front of me, laughing flirtatiously, and not particularly helping the child make better contact.

The arrangement of alternating sessions did bring conflict for Ann. She seemed more contained by the individual sessions to be able to express the most conflictual material. In one she spoke about "a baby killing a man". She played frantically with figures tumbling about in the dolls' house, as she gave me precise accounts of the unfolding story. This story seemed an inversion of the story I was sure she knew somewhere, and perhaps had witnessed, of "a man killing a baby". A related theme in relation to her play was her talking of the television programme *Baywatch*.

Instead of putting the male figure in the chair in the dolls' house to watch the television, Ann had recently begun to put the "little girl" figure in the watching position. I interpreted her "Baby . . . watch" and her worries about what happens to babies.

This work of helping Ann to be allowed to know and experience was so intensive that it spanned each setting in which the child was seen in the hospital. She had different experiences, particularly with nurses and other children with whom she had built up a bond of trust. Some of this material was stirred up *vis-à-vis* Ann's continued visits to her stepfather in prison. This is the nurse's account of the next children-only play session.

> Ann was quiet and subdued. She simply wanted to listen to stories most of the time, with the exception of one specific piece of play with the dolls. In this, Ann put her baby to bed in the playhouse and then a few minutes later brought the baby to the nurse, saying she had woken up, having had a nightmare, a monster had frightened the baby. Ann reassured the baby and put her back to bed. A few minutes later Ann asked the nurse urgently to come and kill a strange man who had woken the baby and frightened her. The nurse asked if it was a burglar. Ann said "Yes", so she and the nurse phoned the police. A few minutes later the nurse asked Ann if the police had been, and she said, "Yes, the policeman killed the man. He fell down a black hole in the floor into the crocodile's mouth, he's dead now and baby's not frightened any more." The child then stopped playing the game and came and sat quietly, looking sad and wanting another story.

Towards the end as rehabilitation and a return to the community was being organized, Ann felt strong enough to fill in some of the missing links in the story. She asked her mother outright one day, "Did daddy kill Helen?" and her mother answered, "Yes, that's right." In the joint session, the mother needed some help to know how the child could have known this.

In her next individual session, Ann got out a set of teddy puppets (hand puppets) and began a game of two babies who were being looked after. The game reached a climax in which one of the babies, while being changed, was "pinched" and "hit" for being naughty, first by the mother and then by the father. I was clearly directed by her as to what role I should take. To begin with, I had to be someone who held the baby when she was not looking after it. Then she reversed the situation, by making me the person who asks her what the baby can do and what should happen to it. The baby was dealt with somewhat roughly and was passive throughout.

A child of her own age was now leaving the hospital community; Ann was upset and beside herself and cried continuously and "hysterically". She settled down only after having been able to talk to the child again on the telephone a couple of days later. It sounded as if Ann needed confirmation that this other child, even though she had left the hospital, was still there—she needed a reassurance that the other child was still alive. This was another real experience of loss, at an affective level, when Ann re-experienced, through this child's leaving, the traumatic loss of a sister-figure. The child had been a playmate and friend in the hospital, with whom she had had many ups and downs, in particular related to Ann's repeated biting behaviour with other children. The child also saw me with her mother for mother–infant sessions and so was a "therapy sibling" too. Thinking about this difficult experience with a sibling, in therapy and in work with her nurse, enabled Ann to move further in her ability to readjust to the traumatic loss and killing of her baby sister.

The family made a successful discharge to the outside community. In the time since discharge, progress has been satisfactory. There has been social service support but no further treatment.

Conclusion

These are two very severe—indeed, extreme—cases in which, until recently, no kind of psychotherapeutic treatment would have been tried. I have attempted to outline a few features in each case which helped to keep the work going and how we attempted to face the severe splitting and underlying destructiveness at work in the patients, how this had to be done openly, and the impact of it borne by both patients and therapists, so that a better side, something new, could emerge. As far as the workers themselves were concerned, such work took its toll and demanded not just personal resources, capacities for containment and reflection, and capacities to set and redefine the boundaries of treatment, but also all the resources of supervision, including nurse–therapist supervision (Tischler, 1986), to prevent splits that could make the workers enact destructive relationships or want to give up in despair. It also required us to bring our work in the hospital together with the work outside, to keep the therapeutic work with the family within a legal framework (Kennedy, 1989, 1997), and to integrate the views of external agencies—the social services, probation, the guardians *ad litem*, other expert consultants, and the High Court.

In the case of Munchhausen syndrome by proxy, we were breaking new ground, since previously such cases had been seen as untreatable (Kennedy & Coombe, 1995; Meadow, 1977). The focus on the child and her mother's interactions with her, which was possible in the mother–infant sessions, and more extensively in the daily interactions of nursing staff with the family, enabled us to know about the possible risks to the child, the effects on her development, and the progress of the mother–infant relationship. I have referred to only a fraction of the work but have tried to show how the most central aspects of this family's overall treatment came jointly into the mother–infant sessions and the work of the therapeutic community. These were the focus on being watched and what is actually happening to the child, on dangerousness and destructiveness, and on the psychotic elements behind the fears of separation. Indeed, I am sure that other central areas of the work—such as the mother's individual psychotherapy and the focal nursing of the family's primary nurse, or the work of community meetings and work groups in the pantry, the supper team, or the "firm" meetings—could equally illustrate the interlinking of central psychoanalytic aspects of treatment (see chapter two; see also C. Flynn, 1993).

In the second case there were elements that were typical of many cases of the treatment of borderline patients at the Cassel Hospital over the years. Susan had shown a capacity to use psychoanalytic psychotherapy, but the everyday reality of her treatment was that she undermined this repeatedly in a thoughtless and destructive, almost psychopathic, way. Again and again her ambivalence about having Ann back with her, which under-mined their progress together, was brought out into the open. There was difficulty, splits, and strain all round at times, in the family and in the workers. Some workers in the hospital felt that Susan's behaviour was too chaotic and her treatment of Ann still thoughtless and sadistic, and that Ann should not be rehabilitated, while others felt that they could see changes, that it was what Ann wanted, and that she was managing. This latter view in effect influenced the change in technique halfway through—to parallel mother–child and child psychotherapy sessions—to help mother and child adjust to each other and also to allow the child to have the fullest possible space within the circumstances to express herself. It also became more important at that point to recognize that bringing mother and child together could produce a negative response in Susan, and sometimes in Ann too, when she gave way to a muddled and passive negativity. But overall it was Ann's tolerance of individual sessions and her wish to have her thoughts and feelings understood that showed her willingness to persevere through the painfulness of the process. In order to overcome her internal trauma, Ann had to be able to know how it could have happened that her baby sister had been killed, but it was impor-tant for Ann to know, too, how thinking in her internal world could get killed off and would need to be re-formed and found. Susan had to face her own responsibility and some of her failing, and indeed she did do this and was capable of deep and genuine guilt and remorse, which she worked through in her individual psychotherapy. She also needed to be able to allow her child to express her feelings, including her anger with her mother and her acceptance of her stepfather's responsibility, indeed to allow her-self to know what happened. Sufficient support and tolerance was needed in the whole inpatient treatment team to survive negative attacks and to create the space for something new to grow be-tween Ann and Susan.

This tolerance of severe infantile projections, of hostility and despair, and the struggle to maintain cooperative work together, not just the technical changes of the inpatient setting, is what makes work towards successful rehabilitation of such families possible and, in the end, enables the workers to survive and to continue to work in a psychoanalytic way.

CHAPTER FIVE

School children in the Cassel community: discovering a place in which to live and learn

Lee Marsden

This chapter focuses on the educational and therapeutic work with children of school age living in the Cassel Community. Therapeutic teaching takes place in the Children's Centre, an area of the hospital where, as its name suggests, the every day needs of children are the focus. Fundamental to this work is the provision of a reliable, predictable setting, where adults can offer opportunities for secure attachments to develop (Bowlby, 1969) and can help children to make sense of their world (Bion, 1962a). Awareness of the interplay between emotions and thoughts, relationships, and cognitive capacities informs our approach to children's learning (Greenhalgh, 1994; Salzberger-Wittenberg, Henry, & Osborne, 1983). This is similar to thinking that underpins educational therapy (Morton, 2000a). Aspects of this philosophy and practice are similar to those of nurture groups, in which small groups of children are offered therapeutic teaching within a mainstream school setting (Bennathan & Boxall, 1996). There is an emphasis on nurture, noticing and responding to even small details of a child's concerns, and behaviour of any kind is understood as a form of communication (Holmes, 2000). Different aspects of this therapeutic teaching are illustrated in the following description of the daily work of the Children's Centre and account of my work as the teacher with two children who were resident at the Cassel and attended the Children's Centre.

The Cassel community

The Cassel Hospital is a therapeutic community, treating adolescents, adults, and families. The Families Unit, one of three units in the hospital, works with parents and children whose functioning as a family has caused extreme concern, with the protection of the children being a key issue. Families come to live as members of the Cassel community, and, after a six-week period of assessment, they may be offered long-term treatment. They arrive with the hope that they can change the ways in which they relate and, in time, return to live in their own communities, either as a more healthily functioning family or, at least, with some understanding of why this is not possible for them and why alternative opportunities need to be created to meet their children's emotional and developmental needs.

Within the Cassel community, everyone—patients and staff—is encouraged to observe his or her own and each other's feelings and behaviour. Discussion, questioning, and debate are constantly fostered. While each patient—child or adult—has his or her own therapist, with whom there is space to work in a more private and confidential manner, therapeutic work of a more public kind takes place through the very ordinary, practical tasks that need to be performed to keep the community running. Nursing staff, who are trained to think and practise psychosocially, work together with patients in cleaning, cooking, caring for children, and undertaking all that is entailed in the everyday business of living together. In performing this ordinary "work of the day" (Kennedy, 1986), patients may draw attention to aspects of themselves and their lives. Nurses can respond to information or feelings as these arise, and they may encourage patients to discuss issues around each other's words or behaviour in both informal and more formally structured contexts.

For children at the Cassel, as for all children, hopefully, the ordinary "work of the day" involves playing and learning. Just as their parents may demonstrate their unhappiness and difficulties in a struggle to prepare a meal on time, or in obsessive care for their rooms, so some children may choose nursery activities or school work as an arena in which to communicate some of their feelings. While the needs of children are carefully observed and considered in the everyday context of the community, they can be more specifically addressed within the Children's Centre, a part of the Families Unit that offers children therapeutic education and activities from Monday to Friday.

The Children's Centre is staffed by a teacher, a nursery nurse, and nurses, all of whom work and think within a therapeutic, psychosocial framework. The Centre is a purpose-built area attached to the main body of the hospital and includes a nursery for pre-school children, two well-equipped classrooms, an art-room, a kitchen, and other flexibly used spaces. These rooms are built around a courtyard garden, and the aim is to provide a calm, containing atmosphere, centred around the children's needs.

The weekly timetable of the Children's Centre provides the structure within which children are offered direct teaching and learning, together with opportunities to reflect on, and make changes to, the ways they experience themselves within an educational setting.

Using information from the child's last school, together with ongoing observation and assessment, the teacher plans individual programmes of study, emphasizing literacy, numeracy, and social skills. These and other subjects may be taught within a topic area that is likely to have appeal and relevance to a wide age group and the possibility of differentiated learning objectives. Individual interest, preoccupations, strengths, and weaknesses are considered in planning how to reach children who may bring with them negative experiences of school and teachers and a need to overcome a sense of failure. Such children may appear uninterested in learning, frightened, angry, and destructive. Alternatively, they may show their hostility through quiet withdrawal. Others may be managing academic work successfully but may be quietly over-compliant or unable to link up with teachers and other adults in ways that allow them to share and develop their knowledge and skills in a mutually satisfying way. Others again may have difficulty in sharing adult attention so that their rivalrous feelings prevent them from getting on with their learning in a normal group or classroom setting.

Whatever the behaviour, the staff are concerned with enabling each child to develop his or her capacities for learning. The curriculum activities and materials are designed to ensure some experience of success and to indicate to the child that the teacher is trying to listen to his or her communications about him/herself as a learner. For example, the reading and writing of appropriate stories can help to address indirectly a child's concerns (Morton, 1996). Thinking together to make and tell stories (Morton, 2000b), to sequence fictitious events, can help the child to make more sense of a personal narrative that may be painful and difficult to piece together clearly. Educational games (Holditch, 1995) and creative expression work (High, 1985) are also used to help children disentangle some of their emotional difficulties from their learning.

Transitional space and attachment

A factor of great importance in the children's ability to engage and participate in the work of the Children's Centre is always their experience within their own family and that family's views and experiences of education, schools, and teachers. The staff of the Children's Centre work with other clinical staff in the hospital community to help parents support their children's schooling. Alternative ways of thinking about and understanding each child's behaviour are considered, so that different ways of responding to or anticipating children's needs can be tried and the children can be given an experience of adults working together to think about them.

Connecting the Children's Centre and the hospital community is a reception area, effectively a transitional space that helps to signify both the link and the boundary between the two. This is where, on arrival at the start of the school day, parents are encouraged to tell staff about any issues or events that may be affecting their children's behaviour or abilities to cope with school work. Similarly, they are asked to listen to, and think about, staff experiences with their children when they are collected from school. This handing on of information in the children's hearing, with some brief ensuing discussion, creates opportunities for children to experience being thought about by parents and staff together and so to feel more held and freer to learn. It can also help parents to be more mindful of their children and more thoughtful about ways in which children's experiences both in and out of school can interact, affecting their emotional life in ways that can influence their capacity for learning (Winnicott, 1964).

As might be expected, however, these moments of separating and reconnecting can also be fraught and difficult. These are families in which there have been a variety of disturbances and disruptions, leading to complex attachment patterns (Ainsworth, Blehar, Waters, & Wall, 1978). Some children and parents may have difficulties in saying goodbye to each other, with children becoming clingy or tearful. One child may ignore his or her own parent, bidding for attention from the parent of another child. A parent whose own child is becoming upset may become too "helpfully" involved in attending to another child's distress. Siblings can become rivalrous about who gets the first/last/biggest hug from a parent. Parents may become competitive with each other in relation to staff attention, or they may direct hostile, rivalrous feelings towards the staff with whom they are leaving their children. Others are barely able to disguise their delight at being able to leave their children in someone else's care.

At this transitional point, there may need to be some negotiation about an object a child wishes to bring in to the centre. Parents may need staff help in reinforcing their authority over the surrender of sticks, stones, and other potentially dangerous items. Some children like to bring all kinds of small toys, soft toys, or comics. The rules and boundaries around the use of such items during the day need to be clearly decided, and staff will also be alert to the possible meanings of some of these objects as expressions of the relationship between child and parent and their own emotional worlds (Winnicott, 1971c). For example, a teddy bear, described by one parent as much loved by a child and likely to be helpful in supporting her through a potentially difficult day, became maltreated and a source of general distraction once in the centre. This gave rise to a discussion that began to disentangle what was an issue for the parent from the issue for the child. Younger children may be expected to have a reading folder that passes between parents and the centre, and attitudes to this by all concerned can be indicative of how effectively we are able to share a commitment to a child's education.

The emotional experience of the classroom

On leaving the reception area, children and staff sit together to discuss any issues that have come up since the previous day, any ongoing matters, and the plan for the day ahead. This can be a difficult time, in which reference may be made to adult disputes, sleepless nights, and all sorts of issues involving painful feelings. It can also be an opportunity for the children to have help in thinking about and processing their experiences both in the hospital community and beyond. It is also a time for children to be together as a distinct group and to think with nurses and the teacher about issues of sameness, difference, and their own individual identities.

The common thread that brings the children of Families Unit patients together in the Cassel is the experience of severe family disturbance. The mix of ages, personalities, gender, and ethnicity has not been selected with either educational or therapeutic aims in mind. For example, there are often siblings within the classroom, and because of their shared life within the hospital, there is something of a sibling quality in the group as a whole. Not surprisingly, therefore, there can be intense feelings, positive or negative, expressed both consciously and unconsciously towards each other and towards staff. The changing membership of the group, as children and their families leave treatment and new children arrive, makes a strong impact, resonating with some children's earlier experiences of changing family composition as well as fears and hopes for the future.

Following the initial session described above, children move to work in the classrooms, perhaps individually, in pairs, or in a small group, depending on the mix of ages, abilities, and interests. Clarity about which staff member they are working with can be very important for some children, as well as for staff, who may need to withstand attempts at splitting or attempts at avoiding connection with any adult. For example, it may happen that a child responds very differently to two staff members. The child may be cooperative and responsive with one of them, while avoiding and denigrating the other one. Staff will try to think with the child about what this may mean and whether such a split offers some understanding of the child's world. The split might appear to relate to professional roles, gender, or something in the child's experience that leads him or her to make one adult carry all the negative feelings towards authority or carers and another to be idealized. Where this is clear, the staff will then work to help the child reach a point where he or she can relate to them more as individuals in their own right, offering a mixture of good and not-so-good qualities. Similarly, in a case where a child attempts to shut off from adult contact, staff will attempt to gain some trust from the child and seek to understand why this is happening.

Planning for each child's individual learning requires careful thought. On the one hand, there needs to be judicious gauging of the child's capacity to respond to direct "curriculum delivery", where the teacher defines the learning task, endeavouring to keep the child on track despite any possible attempts to avoid the work. On the other, there needs to be a receptivity to the child's own preoccupations, requiring staff to adapt, alter, or abandon the activity planned. Such adaptation may come about for a number of reasons. For example, there may be conscious negotiation initiated by the child that enables the teacher and the child to define together a new task. In such cases, the teacher may need to ensure that the new task is one that has shared meaning for them both and is not something that the child controls, shutting off contact with the teacher. Another possibility is that the task may need to be altered because the teacher senses that the child is communicating, perhaps unconsciously, some feelings or preoccupations that need acknowledgement before the curriculum work can be tackled successfully. For example, a small cartoon figure doodled in a margin might be picked up as a character to be developed through a story or cartoon conversation. This character may be able to express for the child feelings or thoughts that the child is unable to express for him/herself directly, or the "character" may be more able to tolerate "listening" to the teacher (Morton, 1996). Sometimes, the repeated humming or singing of a song or phrase from a song may not be intended simply to distract the teacher but may be expressing the child's feelings. Offering an opportunity to record this on tape may allow these feelings to be expressed and then free the child to concentrate more fully on the given task.

The relationship between the emotional experience of the child and his or her capacity to learn is vital, therefore, to our understanding of the difficulties that these children may face. This is explained more clearly in the next section through a discussion of work with two children who were living in the hospital community and attending the Children's Centre.

Fiona and Ian

Fiona, the elder, and Ian were born a year apart. They were the children of mixed parentage, in terms of race, religion, and culture. Mrs Clarke, their mother, had come to Britain as a young school child. During Fiona and Ian's early years, family life was confusing and volatile. Their father left the family when Fiona was about 3 years old, and thereafter he seems to have made erratic and unpredictable appearances in their lives. Other family members significant to the children were also unreliable, and their mother's own disrupted and abusive childhood contributed to her increasing difficulties in parenting the children. Eventually, they came to the attention of social services and were placed in residential care.

By the time Mrs Clarke, Fiona, and Ian were referred by social services to the Cassel, Fiona was 9 years old and Ian was 8. The aim of the admission was to enable Mrs Clarke to meet the children's needs more effectively. Following a period of assessment and treatment, the Families Unit team, together with the referring social services, would make an informed and considered recommendation concerning the children's future.

Prior to the family's admission at the Cassel, phone contact and written reports from Fiona and Ian's teachers gave a picture of how the children were functioning in school. Both were described as lacking confidence. They needed constant reassurance that their behaviour and their approach to their work were acceptable and "correct". Both children had difficulties in making friends, and they relied on each other at playtimes. Ian was described as "a shy, reserved child", Fiona as "a bit of a loner". Although Ian was identified as needing considerable extra support to concentrate on tasks and to develop his fine motor skills, his difficulties in learning were seen as "largely an emotional problem". Fiona was described as hard-working, "very bright and capable of above-average work", but often behind and needing "a life of her own".

Relationship between mother and children

Before the children started working with us, I met Fiona and Ian's mother. It was a confusing meeting in which she was critical of the children's previous school, both the teachers and the other pupils. She gave me a picture of Ian as utterly dependent on her, needing her to shield him from unruly children and unkind teachers, but also capable of enormous anger and aggressive outbursts. She told me that he had been diagnosed as suffering from attention deficit hyperactivity disorder and that this was the cause of his difficulties both in school and at home. During all this, there was no mention of Fiona, and even when I asked directly about her daughter, Mrs Clarke quickly moved the conversation back to Ian. I was already gaining an impression of an enmeshed relationship between Ian and his mother in which struggles of power, dependence, and vulnerability left little room for Fiona's emotional life to exist.

Mrs Clarke also wished to impress on me that, racially and culturally, the children were of mixed parentage. She said she attached importance to observing her own cultural customs and encouraging the children to do likewise. She seemed to be feeling great strain and anxiety at the prospect of possibly not being allowed to leave the hospital to take part in a pending religious festival. I felt that I was being sought as a prospective ally in the event of an anticipated battle over this. It was with some difficulty that I reminded her that we were currently meeting to think about her children's needs, including the important fact that their education needed to take account of their mixed heritage. In an early meeting like this one, finding out about a parent's own childhood experiences of school and teachers can be useful. However, in this instance, I was hesitant to engage with these details, as Mrs Clarke was making me feel overwhelmed by a catalogue of unmet needs that appeared to span her entire life.

As discussed previously, the manner in which children are brought to the Centre and met again can help us to see aspects of the parent–child relationship and the general family dynamic. At points of leaving and greeting, there quickly developed a pattern of relating between Ian, Fiona, and their mother that continued throughout the initial six-week assessment period and for phases well beyond that. All the interaction at these times was between mother and son, while Fiona hovered apparently neutrally at the side or in the background, as if completely dissociated from her mother and brother. Generally, Ian would cling to his mother as she said goodbye at the beginning of the school day, whining anxiously that he did not want to go to school. When they met at the end of the morning or afternoon, he would often greet her with lowered head and drooping shoulders, shrinking into her arms yet seeming to gain little reassurance or comfort from the contact. He became extremely anxious if she kept the children waiting at all at the ends of school sessions.

The nature of the attachment between each of the children and their mother showed marked differences, but, in terms of the attachment patterns described by Ainsworth et al. (1978), both were insecure or anxious (Geddes, 1999). Fiona's emotional distance, combined with her hovering and disguised watchfulness, suggested an anxiously avoidant attachment. It was easy for this pattern to continue alongside the over-close, physically clinging contact between mother and son. This followed a pattern of ambivalent attachment in which the mother's physical contact with her child was more an expression of her own needs than an attempt to understand and respond to the emotional needs of the child. This left Ian with very little space to risk a separate sense of self (Barrett & Trevitt, 1991).

Shared feelings

It was not surprising that, at first, Fiona and Ian found it difficult to engage with any discussion of events or feelings. They found the open acknowledgement of their own and other people's troubling behaviour and emotions painful and threatening. While Fiona attempted to avoid involvement in the morning meetings by silently cutting off and staring into space, Ian's way of protecting himself was to interrupt other people with a semi-coherent flood of chatter. This was sometimes designed to amuse and so change the tenor of the discussion, but sometimes he could be enormously angry in attempting to deflect attention from an issue he did not wish to hear being considered. For example, staff attempts to understand a conflict within the group by unravelling some of the feelings involved might lead Ian to respond as if he or another child were about to be punished. This made it very hard for him to listen to what was actually being said, and it was hard, too, for staff to be clear about the real causes of his anger.

One aspect of the morning meetings that made a strong impact on Fiona and Ian was the realization that adults thought and talked about them even when they themselves were not present. Staff reference to information gained from nurse handovers after the night shift or from staff meetings were often met with an incredulous but generally pleasurable, "How do you know that?" At times, it seemed that they enjoyed playing with the idea that staff could be magically all-knowing. At other times, they made clear their resentment that staff communicated details of events that the children would have preferred to leave unmentioned—for example, arguments among some of the parents on the Families Unit or worries about a fire alarm that had gone off in the middle of the night.

During our discussion times, it also emerged that, despite Mrs Clarke's declared wish for her children to be aware of their mixed heritage, they both found issues of personal or cultural identity almost unapproachable. In particular, Fiona seemed quite oblivious to the concept of a separate, autonomous self, linked either emotionally or culturally with other people. Ian was more able to talk in terms of having a mother who was from a minority culture. However, when offered the opportunity either to explain or to discover more about the culture, his main motivation seemed to be to please his mother and strengthen his already close identification with her. At this point in his development, complexities around personal emotional connections were of greater significance for him, but it was fortunate for both children that they came to develop a warm relationship with a staff member from a similar cultural background. This enabled them to experience some questioning of their emotional worlds and ways of relating, in a manner that also demonstrated empathy with their mother's social and cultural context.

For Mrs Clarke, issues involving personal and cultural loss were inevitably intertwined. Her own difficulties in facing loss had had consequences for her children, further compounded by the family losses they had all experienced prior to arriving at the Cassel. Issues of loss and change, always present in the Children's Centre work, aroused feelings in Fiona and Ian. Despite initial attempts to protect themselves from any acknowledgement of these feelings, they soon showed that they were acutely aware of any changes in the composition of the group or the organization of the day. Staff attempts to anticipate and raise awareness of such changes, however slight, became increasingly important and valued by them, to the point that they could begin to anticipate these and ask more questions for themselves.

Feelings and learning

About four months into treatment, Fiona and Ian experienced another major loss when, without warning, they received the news that their father had died. This occurred soon after they had established a new pattern of regular weekly contact with him. At first, both children were unable to use opportunities within the Children's Centre to speak directly about their father and his death, but a few days after they had received the news Ian was able to use a structured lesson time to express some of his feelings. We were working on punctuating conversation. Ian was clearly too preoccupied to get anywhere near the given task. After acknowledging this, he dictated to one of the nurses an imaginary conversation he wished he could have had with his dead father. This enabled him to give voice to his feelings, while staying within the lesson context and its objectives. The piece ended with: "I want to say goodbye and that I'm very sad." When it was finished, although still sad, he quietly put the writing away and was more able to be part of the ongoing activities.

Some of the work in the Children's Centre is planned around a termly topic. This is intended to appeal to various ages and levels of functioning while also offering the possibility of some relevance to the children's emotional needs. Fiona and Ian arrived towards the end of a term in which the topic was "Myself". For two children with such a poor sense of self, it was painful to see how difficult each of them found it to state preferences, make choices, or assert their right to a turn on something like the cooking rota or in a game. Fiona, in particular, needed constant reassurance that her ideas were approved of. She was cautious, uneasy, and distant. She frequently deferred to Ian's calls on her own or an adult's attention and seemed bound up with him in a rather collusive, symbiotic relationship in which neither was quite free to develop their own thinking. Each was watchful of the other, with quiet smiles and strong eye contact, Fiona appearing both protective and quietly controlling.

It was important, therefore, to ensure that this brother and sister spent at least part of their time in the Children's Centre working on different activities, sometimes in different rooms. At first, this made Fiona seem rather anxious. She moved between being withdrawn and monosyllabic and constant, rapid speech. Everything was still checked out but with few pauses to hear an answer or develop any really meaningful exchange. An activity like cooking could be accompanied by questions, but in the form of a monologue that expected no reply. She had little idea of how to respond to close adult interest in what her thoughts about her work might be, and she seemed both excited and threatened by the possibility of dialogue about it. For example, a page of maths work might be completed adequately, but Fiona seemed to express unease or slight surprise when I showed a wish to understand the process by which she had arrived at her answers. When I asked, "How did you work that out?" her answer would generally be something like, "I just did." The idea of explaining her thinking to me, or possibly even to herself, seemed at first to puzzle her. I was made to feel intrusive both for seeking to understand her approach and for attempting to present her with one of my own. However, she was clearly familiar enough with the idea that there can be more than one way of tackling a maths problem, and she gradually began to enjoy asking me to guess how she had worked out an answer and then to share with me her exploration of different methods. Probably, this seemed safe enough to attempt because maths at this stage has its correct answers that confirm that a strategy has been effective. Sometimes the explanations given to me contained a tone of triumph, especially when it was clear that Fiona had thought of a strategy that had not been obvious to me.

During their early days in the Children's Centre, children are commonly asked to write a story that offers possibilities of expressing something about their feelings and expectations in coming to the Cassel. Not surprisingly, Fiona seemed careful to avoid direct expression of thoughts and feelings in her story. She was given the opening, "A girl was getting ready to go on a journey. She decided to take with her _____". Fiona's continuation was: ". . . a case with a toothbrush, a tube of toothpaste, pyjamas, coat." She continued the story in a similarly prosaic tone. The girl is alone and spends the first half of the story getting on and off buses and trains, which often take a long time to come and therefore involve a good deal of waiting around at stations and falling asleep. She fills in some of the time by buying food and drink for herself as well as a "reading book". The story becomes more hopeful when she meets a friend on the train and they play six games of snap. It emerges that the two girls are going camping with the friend's relations. They eventually get there about three lines from the end, but all that she says about what happens is, "They had a good time and stayed a week. Then they packed up and went home."

In discussing this story with her, I attempted to get Fiona to imagine more of the experience of the camping holiday and what memories of it the friends might take back or later share, but she was noncommittal. When it came to sharing feelings and ideas, the isolated, waiting girl at the beginning of the story was very like Fiona herself. The apparent self-sufficiency and independence felt limited to practicalities rather than freeing her to make use of fresh adventures. By the end of the story, it seemed that this isolating self-sufficiency was all that the girl could return to. She apparently had no sustaining memory of her holiday, with Fiona lacking the imagination to describe her experience of a good time shared with friends. My suggestion that we could use the story to think about using paragraphs as a way of seeing how the story moves along from one event or idea to another met with a more positive response. This was a more straightforward and technical way of working on the story, thinking about correctness and form and avoiding issues of emotional directness.

The day before writing this story, Fiona had been asked to draw a picture of her family doing something together. She drew Ian, herself, and her mother in a boat and explained that they were going along to the end of a river where they would all get out of the boat. They would all get back in and go back the same way to their home. As well as reflecting some of the family's experiences of travelling back and forth between parts of the country, I felt that the explanation of her picture was like her story. There seemed to be no sense of an experience or event that would make the return journey feel any different from the journey there. There was no expectation that this family arriving in their boat at the Cassel was in search of an experience that would help them to sail back with something having changed between them. Nevertheless, I did feel moved by the strength of her wish for the family to be together.

Feeling, learning, and growing

After the initial assessment period, Fiona started part-time attendance at a nearby mainstream school. This is often the pattern for those children who are able to manage within a mainstream environment, and it is made possible through the interest and goodwill of local-authority schools near the Cassel.

Fiona's attendance in mainstream school meant that she was able to participate in parts of the literacy programme with a class of children her own age, and that, generally, her time in the Children's Centre could be spent on other activities. These included swimming, cooking, art work, and horse riding, all of which afford opportunities for developing aspects of literacy, numeracy, or science as well as developing children's confidence, capacity for enjoyment, cooperation, and greater sense of self. Much of the time, one of our aims for Fiona was to develop her expression of her ideas and feelings and some assertion of herself. There was plenty of evidence that, within the Children's Centre at least, she was growing increasingly spontaneous and less passive. She was further supported in developing more direct expression of herself by the weekly group sessions in dance and movement therapy.

At the beginning of the autumn term, when they had been at the Cassel for six months, it was particularly encouraging to see that both Fiona and Ian were full of a wish to share events and experiences from their summer holiday, recounting stories with an animation and enjoyment that indicated some further develop-ment of an emotional life that they could share more appropriately with others. Because of this, I was unable to resist making the teacher's common demand for a written account of "what I did in the holidays". Compared with her early story, which seemed so uneventful and empty, Fiona's new piece was more lively and full and indicated some shift in her capacity to approach a task. She chose to write about her holiday with staff and children from the children's home where she and Ian were still spending weekends. Her final version started:

> "Ilfracombe is an interesting place. There are lots of shops where you can buy loads of great souvenirs. There is a really big harbour where you can go down some steps onto the sand and see a crowd of boats. It is a good place to take photos. A little further down is the sea.

> "I went to Ilfracombe with a group of children. When we were all standing by the wall, we saw some people in special wet suits by an open bit of the sea. They were all running up and jumping into the sea. When they were in the sea, they swam to a rocky place and climbed up all the rocks and back over the bars. The place from where they jumped was about as high as the Cassel or even higher."

The simile suggests that the Cassel itself is a high vantage point from which it is exciting to run, jump into the sea, swim, and climb to the rocks and back again. There is a slight suggestion of risk and

Fiona is still an observer, but there is a strong pull towards active participation in life, with the suggestion that the Cassel might provide the springboard and the secure base from which this could become possible (Bowlby, 1988). The account continues with a description of the "tiny, tiny stones" to be found on the beach, several of which were collected, brought into the classroom, and carefully drawn. In comparison with earlier work, such attention to their individual features showed Fiona's developing capacities for thoughtful observation as well as pleasure in sharing this with others. In general, it felt that unlike the camping holiday of her earlier story, this holiday was one where things happened. Feelings and experiences could be brought back from the holiday, thought about, and described in ways that enabled Fiona to take the risks involved in using language more freely to connect with other people.

The account that Ian chose to write was also about the excitement that can go with risk and near danger. His spoken account and his written plans were particularly incoherent, and when we eventually sorted out together what it was he wanted to say and write, this was the result:

> "I was spinning round. I was upside down. I stopped and went spinning round the other way. I was on the Samurai 99 Ride. The seats are red, the bars are silver, and you can see the trees below you go round and round really fast. The Ride looks like a windmill with five arms. I like it when you are going round really fast but when it stops and you are upside down, that's the bit I don't like. It seems as if it's going to throw you out of the seat. You're upside down while spinning round really fast."

The piece continues with descriptions of more rides where Ian is excited but disorientated, unsure who or what is in control or whether he can stay on. When he finally leaves the rides behind, he is still disorientated, but the excitement has gone and he becomes, instead, flat and resigned:

> "When it was time to leave, the grown-ups wanted another go on Mystic East, so we were late back. We followed the sign-

posts to find the entrance so we could meet each other. The signposts took us to different places and so did the people we asked. Eventually, we got to the entrance and all the other people had gone. The families had to go because the babies and little children were tired and hungry. It was dark and we had to go back to the Cassel on the bus."

For me, this was a vivid expression of Ian's sense of being precariously positioned in the care of adults who put their own needs first, oblivious to his own anxiety and discomfort. He also made clear a wish to be given the consideration of a baby or a little child whose tiredness and hunger are seen as more legitimate demands on adult resources. It reminded me of his early picture of his family together. In this, the two children and their mother are seated on a row of chairs, each with their back to the one behind. They are all reading their own book. Ian is drawn and labelled as a baby, and he is naked. However, on this occasion (working on the writing), despite a strong pull to engage with the feelings of this baby Ian, I was also very aware of his need to develop skills appropriate to the 9-year-old in the classroom. I acknowledged briefly with Ian some of the feelings in the writing and pressed on with the process by which we aimed to come to a final piece of neat work. This went on over several days, and it was probably only when it was completed and displayed on the wall that Ian had an overall sense of the writing process we had gone through together. An important by-product of this was, I believe, his awareness that together we had made some sense of his excited, confused, and painful feelings.

A secure base for learning

During Fiona and Ian's second school term at the Cassel, our topic was "Buildings". This was inspired partly by the visibly growing new Families Unit building. Thinking about the materials involved in the new building provided a basis for some science and technology work, and the contrast with the older parts of the hospital helped to develop some historical thinking. This linked in with the possibility of exploring very many buildings of interest in the area. Quite often, this topic gave rise to discussions about shelter, comfort, protection, safety, containment, and so on, and it was noticeable how often these issues were linked with their feelings about the Cassel.

In connection with the Buildings topic, I introduced the story from *Grimm's Fairy Tales* of "The Fisherman and His Wife". In this well-known tale, the fisherman's wife wishes that they could live in a comfortable cottage instead of their poor hut. The wish is granted by a magic fish. The wife then wishes for increasingly rich and sumptuous homes together with personal power and wealth. The plot is simple and predictable, but this story, like so many fairy tales and stories, lends itself to a variety of meanings and themes for different children (Green, 1996). We read the story together, and then each of the children in the group chose an aspect of the story to draw or model. The various houses and palaces were obvious choices, but there was also interest in the magic fish, the palace guards, the unpredictable sea, and the wish of the fisherman's wife to be all-powerful.

Ian and Fiona were both drawn to making models of the most lavish and splendid of the palaces or castles. As they worked, they spoke openly of the Cassel itself as if it were a splendid castle. As well as being suggested by its name, this idea was prompted by the nature of the hospital building, an old and rambling house with many staircases, corridors, and rooms, a few of which were mysteriously private and inaccessible, but most of which was theirs to discover and explore. The particular castles they were modelling became less connected with the story of the fisherman and more representative of their feelings about the Cassel as a place full of wealth and riches in which they had some rightful share and played an active part. It seemed as if the Cassel building represented for them also the whole community, with many significant people among the patients and staff. They shared with me their highly detailed knowledge of the workings of the Cassel community: the moves made by nurses from one unit to another, even before they themselves had arrived; the length of time several long-standing members of staff had been there; places that people were moving to; which patients had once been in which room, and so on. Their grasp of this complex institution and their pleasure in unravelling it struck me forcibly when, following their father's funeral, they tried to talk about some of the relatives at the service, some of whom they seemed to have met for the first time. We tried to draw up a family tree to clarify some of the family relationships. It was confusing and distressing for them to face how little they understood of people and events within their own family.

Retreating

After the family had been at the Cassel for about seven months, it seemed that Mrs Clarke herself was continuing to have difficulties in making sense of her own life experiences. It seemed that she would not be able to make effective use of the treatment here, in ways that would support her future parenting. Following a court decision that the children should be fostered but maintain some relationship with their mother, Mrs Clarke returned to her own home. The children moved back to living full time in the children's home, pending placement with a foster-family.

During the day, Fiona and Ian continued to attend the Cassel Children's Centre and, in Fiona's case, the local school. They also continued their own individual-therapy sessions at the Cassel. The continuity and consistency that the Cassel, the children's home, and the school could provide were important in helping the children to process what was happening and what was being considered for their future. Nevertheless, there was a significant shift in the nature of Fiona and Ian's relationship with the hospital community. Ian's experience of this as another loss was clear in his frequently pausing to play with one of the model castles as he walked past. He sometimes pushed the door shut—"so that no one can get out"—or he opened it—"to let somebody back in". One day, I pointed out that this castle had no windows, so no one could see in or out. I wondered if Ian wanted to create some in the cardboard model. At the time he said no and then later wished he had a cardboard box big enough to climb into, like a house, with lots of other little houses inside with him.

This wish to retreat into some secure womb coincided with plans for Ian to begin part-time attendance at the local school. The arrival at the Cassel of a new child, talking with interest about the school she had just left and of her uncertainties about the strange place she had just come to, provided a helpfully wider dimension to our discussions about how different it can feel to be in a larger school and classroom. In fact, I found that I was able to praise Ian's increased ability to reflect on his behaviour within the group, to listen better to others, and to accept the help he still needed with this. At the same time, he was able to let his therapist know that he feared I might be losing sight of his anxieties about school and children who might tease or bully and leave him to struggle alone.

With this in mind, I was able to make use of books related to that term's topic which was "Play". The story of "The Velveteen Rabbit" (Williams, 1992) starts with a toy rabbit arriving in a Victorian nursery. Many of the other toys are mechanical, and, together with other more modern toys, they consider themselves superior to the rabbit. They reject and bully him. Our initial reading included a sentence opening, "Between them all, the poor little Rabbit was made to feel himself very insignificant and commonplace. . . ." Ian commented, "You're reading it as if it's a sad story." This led to discussion of the vocabulary and other possible words for how the rabbit was feeling, with suggestions for how he might manage his feelings and change the situation.

Another book we looked at during this term was *Alice Through the Looking Glass*, by Lewis Carroll. The schools' video and the book offer many possible ways into a child's view of his or her world, while developing educational skills linking with various areas of the curriculum. As part of the Play topic, we were playing several board games, and Ian had become particularly keen on chess. He was fascinated that the story of *Alice Through the Looking Glass* is played out on a huge chess board, with the characters as chess pieces. He struggled to understand the surreal fantasy world of the book, with its many opinionated and bossy characters that try to confuse Alice with their nonsensical logic. Some of this confusion was perhaps too close to his own experience for him to see it as humorous. But, in playing games like chess, both Ian and Fiona had opportunities to understand that at the Cassel, as elsewhere, there are adults who wish not to confuse children. Instead, they try to help make sense, to explain and uphold the rules. The chess games between brother and sister also allowed some safer expression of their rivalry, generally held at bay at a time when their future's only certainty was that they would have each other. In challenging others, they faced the fact that sometimes you win, sometimes you lose, but also that not all games depend on chance alone. Thinking ahead, planning strategically, especially with appropriate adult help, can mean a more favourable outcome, enabling the child to feel less helpless and passive (Holditch, 1995).

In mid-air

During the next term, staff of the Cassel, the local school, and the children's home worked together to support Fiona's and Ian's sense of themselves as two individuals with opportunities for developing and learning. This was difficult to sustain with the uncertainty over how long they might have to wait before a suitable foster placement was found. Our topic during that term was "Time", and as the anniversary of these children's arrival in the Cassel came and went, it seemed that much was being expected of them.

At the time of writing, Fiona and Ian are in the middle of yet another school term. Our topic is "Changes". They see other children and staff come and go, but they are still waiting to hear more about the plan for their own futures. Both children are now attending the local school for a substantial part of the week, and, while school can still evoke their feelings of emotional and social vulnerability, it offers them some sense of continuity and predictability. In their different ways, both children manage to sustain some wish to learn, supported by opportunities to express and understand an immensely complex range of feelings arising from their situation. But there is also growing concern that the children's own active moves towards change could lose momentum, and, returning to Fiona's image, I am sometimes fearful that the two children may feel left in mid-air, unsure of where they will land. However, the implied image is of the Cassel as a point from which to jump off and swim. What stays in my mind is that the children return many times to repeat the jumping and swimming, the risk and the struggle. This emphasizes how important it is to maintain for these children some hope for their future.

Staff feelings

Needless to say, my own changing feelings about Fiona and Ian, and about the situation they are now in, are those of only one involved professional. The conflicting feelings and frustrations felt by staff in such circumstances can lead to a sense of guilt or a wish to apportion blame to one or other section of the professional network. This is exacerbated by the frustration of family members who at different times wish to direct their anger towards an individual worker or a particular group of workers, such as Children's Centre staff, teachers, social services, psychotherapists, or nurses. The wish to blame is further compounded by such realities as staff changes and departures, which may necessitate practical changes in routines and working alliances but also give rise to a tangle of personal feelings in both families and staff.

For these reasons, an important aspect of work in the Children's Centre is the exchanging and processing of staff views and feelings. This takes place through daily staff meetings for the core team and other regular meetings with psychotherapists, family nurses, and the entire Families Unit staff. All of these will have their own perspective on the workings of the family dynamic and, in their different ways, contribute to the understanding of the feelings aroused in the team, which is particularly helpful to those individuals most closely or intensely involved with a family member. In sharing our own feelings about the children and their families, both formally and informally, we have opportunities for gaining greater clarity about a family's predicament. We can also become more effective in understanding and reducing the inevitable tensions that arise in any multidisciplinary team and in strengthening our working relationship with outside agencies such as social services and local schools (Obholzer & Roberts, 1994).

Conclusion

Every child's time at the Cassel has its own story line, in which Cassel staff and patients become closely and sometimes intensely involved. The staff attempt to be mindful of each child's current concerns, as well as hopes for the future and links with aspects of the past. Naturally, we speculate on how each one may come to view this phase of their lives, but the hope is that the experience of living and learning at the Cassel will have contributed to some increased understanding of themselves, on which they can build within their own communities.

CHAPTER SIX

Adolescence: a transitory world

Kevin Healy

I n this chapter, I explore adolescence as a transitory world, drawing upon psychoanalytic writings on adolescence and transience. The psychoanalytic and psychosocial principles underlying the treatment programme for adolescents at the Cassel Hospital are discussed. Consideration is also given to the impact on those who work and live with young people for whom this transitory period is a troublesome and distressing one. Clinical material is used to highlight the transitions of adolescence relating to identity, attachment, sexuality, and the inner phantasy lives of young people.

Adolescence and transitions

Adolescence is a time of transitions. The *Oxford Reference Dictionary* defines "transit" (from the Latin, *transire*, to go across) as a process of going, conveying, or being conveyed across, over, or through. "Transition" itself is defined as the process of changing from one state or subject to another. The adjective, "transitory" is defined as the quality of "not lasting or existing; only for a time". This terminology is very relevant to the journey of adolescents from childhood to young adult life. Donald Winnicott, psychoanalyst and paediatrician, developed the concept of a transitional object in childhood (Winnicott, 1951). The transitional object helped the child move from a state of being dependent on another person in partial or incomplete ways, which he called "relating", to a state of "using" others more fully, in line with emotionally known and experienced wishes and needs. In their journey through adolescence, young people may create individually or collectively a range of transitional objects to help them on this journey. I suggest that peer relationships, the first loves of adolescence, the culture of adolescence (whether music, art, or rebellion), and the use of legal or illegal substances are transitional objects that help on this emotional journey.

Adolescence is not always a time of angst and turmoil. Rutter and Rutter (1993) have highlighted the dangers of assuming that the issues that arise in the treatment of disturbed adolescents can be generalized to all adolescents. However, this is not to deny the impact of major biological, psychological, and social changes that are central to the transitory world of the adolescent.

The idea of adolescence as a prolonged transitional phase seems to be very much a twentieth-century phenomenon (Anderson & Dartington, 1998). Adolescence is one of the most radical of all the developmental periods. In the few years between the onset of puberty and adulthood one's sense of oneself must adapt to the physical changes of size, build, shape, strength, appearance, and being sexually mature. For boys, this means being able to impregnate and an exponential increase in strength, and for girls to carry a pregnancy, to have breasts, and to menstruate. The social and psychic corollaries of this are to develop the capacity to become intimate with others, to form sexual relationships, to become less dependent on parents, and to move towards separation from the family. Adolescents will also have to survive the modern initiation of manhood and womanhood, completion of their education, and hopefully securing a job—in short, to move towards becoming an independent person both internally and externally. If the adolescent is successfully to achieve adulthood, he or she must renegotiate every aspect of relationships with him/herself and with external and internal objects, in a new context.

Freud used the term "adolescence" in his studies of hysteria (Freud, 1895d). Freud supplied two case histories, one of Frau Emmy von N, the second of Katharina, both young women and both referred to as adolescent. However, the theoretical background to an understanding of adolescence was developed by Breuer in this jointly authored book. As part of his work on anxiety neurosis, Freud wrote briefly of adolescent anxiety (1895b [1894]). There are few other references to adolescence in his collective works.

In his essay on "transience", Freud argued against the notion that all that is loved and admired seems to be shorn of its worth by transience, which is its doom (Freud, 1916a). On the contrary, he argues, transience value is scarcity value in time. Limitation in the possibility of an enjoyment raises the value of the enjoyment. These ideas were formed before the onset of the First World War, a war that shattered pride in the achievements of civilization, admiration for many philosophers and artists, and hopes of a final triumph over the differences between nations and races. It revealed "our instincts in all their nakedness, and let loose the evil spirits within us which we thought had been tamed forever by centuries of continuous education by the noblest minds. It showed us how ephemeral were many things that we had regarded as changeless" (Freud, 1916a, p. 307). Freud does not anywhere link these important concepts to adolescence. It is, however, possible to imagine him arguing that the transience of adolescence should not diminish its importance and may lead to greater interest from others in the phenomena associated with adolescence.

Throughout his writings Donald Winnicott emphasized the inherent potential for growth in individuals, and he developed the concept of the good-enough mother and environment, the concept of the stage of concern (an alternative concept to Klein's depressive position), and the concept of transitional phenomena (Winnicott, 1951, 1963b, 1968a). In particular, Winnicott wrote of the transitional objects of childhood and their place in the development of the child. Transitional phenomena continue to be a feature in all our lives as ways of linking between two states of being. For those of us interested in the worlds of psychoanalysis and psychotherapy, our own personal experiences of our own therapy may serve as a good introduction to transitional phenomena.

Winnicott wrote several papers specifically on adolescence. In his paper, "Hospital Care Supplementing Intensive Psychotherapy in Adolescence" (1963b), Winnicott wrote of adolescence as a phase in healthy growth where defiance is mixed with dependence. He suggested that it was no easy thing and that there was only one cure for adolescence—the passage of time. He suggested that there was much that could be said about the management of care of disturbed adolescents. However, he picked out one thing for special mention: "*There will be suicides.*" He introduces the term "adolescent doldrums" (1961) to describe the few years in which each individual has no way out. In this phase the child does not know whether he or she is homosexual, heterosexual, or narcissistic. There is no established identity, and no certain way of life that shapes the future. There is not yet a capacity to identify with parent figures without loss of personal identity.

In his paper, "Contemporary Concepts of Adolescent Development and Their Implications for Higher Education" (1968b), Winnicott goes on to develop the concept of adolescence as a long tussle to be survived. He suggests that growing up means taking the parents' place and that rebellion belongs to the freedom that parents have given to their children. He states that the adolescent is immature; immaturity is an essential element of health at adolescence. He advises society, for the sake of adolescents and their immaturity, not to allow them to step up and attain a false maturity, by handing over to them responsibility that is not yet theirs, even though they may fight for it. He concludes that the main thing is that adolescence is more than physical puberty, though largely based on it. Adolescence implies growth, and this growth takes time, and while growing is in progress, responsibility must be taken by parent figures. If parent figures abdicate, then the adolescents must make a jump to a false maturity and lose their greatest asset: freedom to have ideas and to act on impulse.

Psychoanalytic principles and practice

Susie was 16 years old, placed in a social services secure unit. She cut herself, overdosed, was violent, and lashed out at herself and others. She used her body promiscuously. She had hung herself a number of times, and at the time of her referral to the Adolescent Service at the Cassel, we were told that she was being restrained by staff up to five times a day. I shall follow through on Susie's story as I explore some of the psychoanalytic principles that guided our work with her at the Cassel.

What happened at the secure unit had been repeated over and over in Susie's lifetime. She had been "looked after" since she was 3 years old and had had a succession of placements in children's homes, foster homes, and a therapeutic community, all leading to breakdowns. There were usually scenes of violence, leading to her exclusion from the setting, and her being moved on to somewhere else. Susie herself was able to explain an incident of violence on the basis of somebody annoying her, somebody saying something they shouldn't have, or somebody taking something of hers. She felt she was only asserting her rights. This may have been her conscious way of understanding what was actually happening at any particular point. However, the word "secure" actually had a lot of meaning at an unconscious level for her. As we got to know more about Susie, we found that there was a sense of security engendered in her when someone else could sit and try to control the violent rages that she faced within herself. There was a sense of security when people restrained her, held her, and took responsibility for what was within her. However, for much of the time this was "known" at a more unconscious level by Susie.

Attempting to understand the meaning of actions can be an intense process. It can be painful and difficult and may itself stir up more disturbed behaviour. However, it is usually helpful for an individual to have some sense of why they do what they do, and to be able to think about themselves, rather than just act without the capacity to think. It is almost always helpful for families and friends to have some sense of what is going on when a loved one is behaving in a strange way. The process of grieving is an example that we all know about. Understanding grieving makes it possible for others to live through it with us. For professionals working with disturbed young adults, understanding does provide a framework in which to continue to be in contact with an individual whose disturbance may be very severe and worrying. A sense of understanding can often make possible what Winnicott termed "holding" (1966) and Bion (1962a) named "containing".

Anxiety is a feature of life that is contained and managed in different ways at different stages of life. Physical discomfort, the fear of falling apart, and other specific anxieties of infancy are usually contained by a "good-enough" environment or environmental mother, who is preoccupied with her child's welfare (Winnicott, 1971a). Bion (1962b) has written of the importance of the containing of a child's distress by another, who can take on board that distress, not be overwhelmed by it but provide a thoughtful and relieving response in return.

What are the anxiety-making issues that face adolescents? The main work of adolescence is trying to discover an identity. This occurs in the external world in terms of career plan and finding a place within a peer group and friends, and it is evident within the increasingly intimate and sexual relations that are now possible. Alongside this is the search for identity within oneself. It is a time when a sense of identity can be fickle and unstable.

Feelings are often intense. Adolescents are moving from particularly intense attachments to family and establishing new attachments with friends and with intimate sexual partners. Moving away from the family and establishing oneself in a larger world is a major cause of anxiety. Adolescents often have many doubts about their sexuality following on the reawakening of sexual feelings early in adolescence. The period of adolescence is both a difficult and also a very exciting time. There is much to be thought about, the world is at their feet, and in one sense everything is still before them. How will an adolescent deal with feelings of love, hate, and aggression? The internal world of the adolescent remains a rich world of fantastical imagery.

Relationships do provide containment for all of us. Most of us get our containment through families, parents, children, friends, peers, colleagues, or loved ones. Disturbed adolescents often rely on professional workers for some sort of containment. Susie was at times "kept alive" by her social worker, who worked alongside her very intensively for a number of years. He was the one who was there from placement to placement to pick things up, to hold things, to be around, and to provide some thinking space around her. Therapeutic relationships provide a setting within which, in the transference, there is a re-enacting or repetition of themes that have arisen from past relationships for an individual. Susie, for example, expected to be rejected all the time. This had been the pattern in her life and was what she often elicited in her current relationships.

Exploring the countertransferential feelings elicited in workers in response to Susie's behaviours and interactions led to a fuller understanding of Susie's psychological world. The exploration of such feelings is a central part of the "culture of enquiry" at the Cassel Hospital, which makes possible psychological work with disturbed and disturbing individuals.

It can be very painful and traumatic to get in touch with the traumas of another person's life. As clinicians we need to be sure of our own containment for the therapeutic work that we do, in order to be clear about the management structures of our organization and that we have adequate supervision. We need to have space just to share with colleagues when we have had a difficult time. Many of us work within teams and/or institutions and are reliant on others within the institution to provide an overall thinking space within the organization.

The work of adolescence

Winnicott (1971b) has described playing as the work of childhood. The child will often create its own fantasy world and enact and live through important developmental issues through such play. The imagery involved is largely conscious, with important unconscious elements attached. In contrast, in the world of adults, we work in the "real world" of employers, businesses, finances, mortgages, promotion, redundancy, retirement, success, failure, and so forth. Much of what determines our involvement in this world, I suggest, is largely unconscious, with significant conscious elements attached. Following on the work of Bion, Stokes (1994) has written of valencies in each of us that draw us towards our particular area of work. For example, those of us struggling with a basic issue of dependency may well end up as doctors, nurses, or in other care-giving roles. Those of us struggling with basic issues of fight or flight may seek more confrontative roles in our work career. Those of us influenced by basic issues of pairing may end up as therapists working individually and intensively with our clients. Most of us, however, are not conscious of these particular reasons for choosing the careers we follow. We can give all sorts of conscious, practical, and pragmatic reasons why we do what we do and why we have followed the path to our particular work identity.

I suggest that the adolescent lies somewhere in the middle between childhood and adulthood, between living in a world of fantasy and living in a world of reality. The adolescent may achieve this difficult position by being able to live for some time within a transitory but real world of adolescent sub-culture. It is not an easy position to hold: the adolescent is buffered by the regressive calls of childhood functioning and the "progressive pushes" to possible premature adult functioning. Adolescence is usually a very difficult time for all of us, including those of us who have had a stable family life, adequacy of material comforts, or what Winnicott termed a good-enough environment. For those who have struggled with privation or deprivation, who have not known the stability of family life, the warmth of a loving, caring parent, or the comfort of close siblings, these struggles can be overwhelming. Yet such a disturbed background is usual among those adolescents assessed and treated on the Adolescent Service at the Cassel Hospital. I shall shortly go on to give some clinical illustrations to illustrate the struggles of this particular group of adolescents, and their attempts to live with their difficulties. Before doing so, I shall sketch out how the organization of the Cassel inpatient setting accommodates the adolescent's transitory world.

The setting of the inpatient work

The Adolescent Service at the Cassel Hospital was set up specifically to cater for the clinical needs of 16- to 21-year-olds who fell between child and adult services. The inpatient psychotherapeutic community is comprised of the Families Unit, the Adult Unit, and the Adolescent Unit, which together form the working therapeutic community. Patients come for treatment at times in their lives when they are feeling desperate, despairing, hopeless, self-destructive, and suicidal. They will often have harmed themselves, or others, in a number of serious ways and are usually very stuck in their lives on referral. All who come to work in treatment must have a wish to risk facing change and to begin to look at and explore their emotional and social worlds.

There are three main strands to the treatment that I believe are of help to adolescents in risking change. First, there is an emphasis placed on relationships formed during treatment. Adolescents will share a room with two or three other young people and will come to know the other adolescents, the adult patients, the parents, and, often importantly, the children with whom they share their lives during the working week. They will build a relationship with their psychosocial nurse, who works closely alongside them on day-to-day issues, planning for times at home over weekends and for the longer term when they leave the hospital. They will also form relationships with their individual therapists, who will see them for two 50-minute sessions each week, and with a group therapist and senior nurse, who will see them for two 1-hour group-therapy sessions each week. Within all these relationships they can expect to repeat all the difficulties they have had up to now in relating. This in itself is not therapeutic but is a first step towards thinking about their difficulties, exploring them, coming to understand them, and seeking ways to change them within the relationships formed.

The second main therapeutic factor is the emphasis placed on adolescents remaining responsible for themselves throughout their treatment. They will be responsible for taking the risks involved in beginning to talk about themselves at their own pace, for keeping themselves safe throughout their treatment, and for allowing others to work alongside them to ensure their safety when they feel at particular risk of harming themselves or others. As treatment progresses, they will be responsible for taking on important jobs within the therapeutic community. These jobs may be of a practical nature, such as preparing meals, keeping the hospital tidy, or running various activities. Patients' jobs also include taking on roles within the Adolescent Unit and within the whole hospital community. They will chair meetings and act as the responsible person to whom other distressed patients may initially go to for support.

The third main therapeutic factor is the emphasis on adolescents getting on with life and facing the ordinary things in living, no matter what else is going on for them. In this way, adolescents are encouraged to develop their particular skills and hobbies and to continue with their education and training. They are also encouraged to carry on with the commitment they have to themselves and to others, no matter what else may be troubling them or distracting them at that time. Life on the Adolescent Unit at the Cassel Hospital is intense and difficult, but at times it can be fun. Patients live in the hospital from Sunday to Friday, returning to their own home at weekends in order to continue to build their lives outside hospital. Patients must make a continuing commitment to their treatment and can at any time choose to leave if that is what they wish. Most patients do not choose to leave and often have few viable alternatives. What keeps most people in treatment at the Cassel Hospital is their recognition that it is usually life-changing and enables them to get beyond the log-jam in their lives, to develop significant relationships for themselves, and to build some future career for themselves. Family work is an integral part of the treatment provided. Linking with the many professionals involved in the lives of these adolescents is a crucial part of the treatment package, as it helps to integrate the input of the workers, which often reflects the emotional state of the adolescent.

The "culture of enquiry" is evident in the above description. Through enquiry, difficult experiences come to have meaning and can then be expressed in thoughts, and perhaps in words, as a way of avoiding the urge to repeat such experiences within current relationships and situations. Such a shift represents a huge step for the adolescent in treatment. Troubled adolescents often feel very stuck in their development, and this shift reflects a freedom within the adolescent and the rediscovery of the capacity to be creative. Adolescence is often a time of great creativity. Their attention is drawn to relationships outside of family and to the world at large. It is a time of discovery for all concerned, and no less so for those of us who work with adolescents. Adolescence is a transitional space that maintains contact with the world of childhood and with the world of adult responsibility. Each of us, perhaps, could benefit from continuing to live or lives within such a transitional world, where access to our inner life can allow us to impose significant meanings on to the outside world with which we interact.

Clinical examples

Finding an identity

Since running away from her family one year previously, Mary had sixteen placements and several assessments in various treatment facilities. She was referred to the Adolescent Unit after other attempts to treat her had broken down. Mary was an emotionally damaged young woman, who described having been sexually abused by her father for many years. She herself abused substances, mutilated herself by cutting, and had attempted to strangle herself more than once. Mary's surname and address were unknown. She had refused to disclose this information to any of her carers. There appeared to have been a rivalrous relationship between Mary and her older sister for the major place in their father's affections. At the age of 14, Mary ran away to London, hoping that life would be better and safer for her. Instead, she found herself on the streets, cold, frightened, and abusing any substance she could get hold of. When she first came to the attention of social services, she had been found unconscious after sniffing glue in a London train station.

Mary's physical appearance was striking. Her left arm was heavily scarred from repeated self-cutting. She constantly carried a teddy bear with her. She needed to use crutches to get around to support her knee, which had been dislocated during an attempt to restrain her from harming herself in a previous hospital. In her treatment, at times Mary received enormous input and support from other patients and staff. She found this support very containing, yet this often meant that in the process she became more childlike in herself. Her greatest difficulties were in contributing and giving to others. She found it impossible to take on ongoing responsibilities within the therapeutic community. The break-down in this area left her feeling overwhelmed by ongoing explo-ration of her past abusive relationships and unable to contain inevitably difficult feelings.

Mary had decided that all men were bad. If she were going to have relationships, they would have to be with women. She couldn't understand why she had a male pop group poster on her wall, or why she trusted her male nurse. These sorts of confusions often filled her mind and made her uncomfortable. She could be far more comfortable when things seemed clear-cut, either good or bad. She began to think about her confusion of love and hatred for her father. This made her feel terrible about herself.

Mary clearly had major identity problems. She had given up her place in the real, external world, going by a false name with no trace of her background. She moved from acute placement settings to acute psychiatric settings without forming any ongoing rela-tionships. She was not in school, in training, or working towards any career or future. Her use of crutches made it appear as if she "hadn't a leg to stand on". Her internal world was in a mess. She recognized that her great neediness often provoked abusive re-sponses in others. She seemed comfortable at times with such relationships, as if that was the best she could expect for herself.

Dealing with sexuality

Caroline was referred for treatment because of ongoing serious depression and suicidal acting-out. She was the only child of elderly parents. Caroline's depression dated from the age of 11 years. During the early months of Caroline's admission, she often spoke of wanting to leave treatment. Her therapist found it very difficult to have an emotionally alive sense of her and found herself mechanically bringing her up in staff meetings so as to try and keep her in mind somehow. Little by little, Caroline described her role in her family. She saw herself as a kind of partner and protector of her father, who, she felt, was a victim of her mother's cruelty. She would beg them to just listen to each other. She saw herself as the glue that held them together. Seeing her parents in this way was also the glue that held her together by allowing her to project any emotional mess into them. When she felt herself to be sacked from this position, her life became intolerable. Her mother changed towards her father and became more concerned and caring as he had developed a serious, life-threatening illness one year previously. She felt terribly betrayed by her father, who turned towards her mother more. She was furious with both parents and filled with hatred and contempt for them. There was an increasing sense of desperation in her therapy sessions. As she began to value her treatment and to realize her dependence on it, she felt vulnerable and unprotected by her superiority and cold-ness. There were times when she felt herself to have absolutely nothing inside and felt herself to be "a discharge, an angry, stink-ing mess".

Along with this increased vulnerability and anxiety came mo-ments of increasing warmth towards particular friends and rela-tions. This gave her some hope that her internal coldness might not last forever. As she became more engaged in her treatment in the hospital, she also took more risks for herself. She used her sessions to think about and experience herself in a different way. She talked with other patients, and in group sessions, in a more open way about herself. She took on a variety of jobs within the inpatient therapeutic community that allowed her to exercise both responsibility for herself and an ownership of her own thoughts, feelings, and actions. She became more able to express her anger and disagreement, her warmth, and, increasingly, her sexuality. She experimented with her life and took some risks that would allow her to experience fresh situations. Just as with her school work as a young teenager, she also "cheated" within the hospital. She stayed up late at night talking into the small hours with some male patients. She experimented with some vodka that another patient had brought into the hospital, against hospital rules. She became much more aware of her impact on others and was both provocatively sexual at times and provocatively stubborn at oth-ers. She risked being more openly hostile to her parents and would often not let them know until the last minute whether or not she would be returning home to them for her weekends away from the hospital. She had the option also of staying with a favourite older female cousin whom she had also begun to treat in the same way. In one sense she was positively asserting herself as an individual but was unable to do this in a way that left others feeling satisfied on her behalf.

Impact on others

I have wished to stress and make clear in the examples given above that the lives of these particular adolescents are highly charged and full of intense, rawly expressed emotion. I have omitted the therapeutic interventions aimed at helping the adolescent make sense of these transient raw emotions. All those who come in contact with these young people will undoubtedly be affected. Some will allow the emotional world of disturbed adolescents to impact on their lives in a direct way; others, because of the need to protect themselves from intolerable anxieties, will find ways to defend against the rawness of these relationships. Most of us will move between such ways of relating.

I want to emphasize two points here. First, as mentioned earlier, not all adolescents experience such emotional intensity or repeat such emotional traumas within their relationships (Rutter & Rutter, 1993). The adolescents described in this chapter come from a highly selected group of individuals who have needed the containment of inpatient treatment, within a therapeutic community, to help them safely on their journey through adolescence. Their behaviours are extreme, their emotions are very raw, and their impact on others is immense. We need to recognize, however, that each adolescent must find his or her own way of living with the intensity, rawness, and turmoil. Second, I wish to emphasize that, within the setting described, adolescents often have their most intense relationships with each other, and consequently their impact on each other can be immense. In this section, however, I want to emphasize the impact on staff working with such adolescent disturbance.

Helping staff to survive emotionally is essential for this work to continue. This psychological survival needs to happen on a day-to-day basis and over time if effective work with patients is to continue and staff burn-out is to be avoided. Containment for staff is built into the working structures of the Adolescent Unit. Above all, it depends on the quality of relationships established and on the line management and supervisory capacity within the staff team. Supporting staff is facilitated through allowing feelings to be heard. Use is then made of these feelings to explore the psychodynamics of the interaction between adolescents and staff. Such an understanding develops within individual supervision, within joint supervision with nurse and therapist of a particular adolescent, and within the daily staff meetings involving all staff as available on the Adolescent Unit. In such settings we are very aware of the process of splitting, and we use the fact that workers often experience very polarized feelings in relation to a patient to understand the dynamics of that patient which engage us. Being aware of these dynamics is usually helpful in bringing the world of the patient together. Treatment usually means that patients will re-enact situations from their internal world and from their past and will test staff as to whether they can hold concern for the patient when all feel so despairing. Holding suicidal feelings can be easier when these are openly shared with other workers and thought about together. It is very important that one person is not filled up with all the anxiety on behalf of the team.

When primary workers are absent, it is important that the patient actually knows who is going to be keeping them in mind and looking after them. Issues of clear authority are usually very significant within the staff team and are sometimes severely tested through the re-enactment of difficulties from an adolescent's internal world (Menzies Lyth, 1979). The management by senior nurse and consultant psychotherapist of the Adolescent Unit needs to allow a space for autonomy for the patient, for their key primary workers, and for the staff group as a whole to make autonomous and considered judgements. Against this background of respect for individuals' rights, some clear limits around what behaviours are unacceptable within the hospital need to be set and maintained. The role of the nurse at the Cassel Hospital is to work alongside patients and to interact and be with patients in an everyday way. Because of the support that is available, nurses on the unit are able to engage in relationships with patients that would be intolerable in a less supportive setting. Working as a psychosocial nurse is extremely demanding in a personal and professional way. Nurses expose themselves to all sorts of intense feelings directed towards them by the patient in order to be able to work effectively towards change. Nurses do not deny their patients' stress and disturbance, but encourage patients to explore alternative ways of managing this disturbance through developing and using everyday relationships for effective support.

John's story

I want to end this chapter by describing John's transition through the Cassel Adolescent Service. This description is both the story of John and the story of the treatment programme at the Cassel.

John was a 20-year-old adolescent living with his guardian. When I met with him he struck me as tall and neatly dressed, and he wore a Walkman around his neck to the interview. He arrived half an hour late for our appointment, blaming the trains and the buses, and commented that it was a very cold day. He told me that outpatient counselling had not been enough for him, and he felt he was now stuck and back at square one. He talked of going to an art college and of his interest in painting. He had not been impressed with others on the course there. He felt that they thought they were geniuses, but they threw paint at canvases, often creating "chaotic mess". He himself would have preferred some order to this. He liked to set limits and a structure for himself. He spoke of a particular task at college when he was asked to describe himself in images without actually drawing himself. He felt annoyed that others tried to create images of themselves by drawing pictures of their families—"parents, two children, and a cat". This enabled us to consider more about himself and his family. He had felt very central in his own family. John was the one who talked with the doctors at the age of 16 when his mother was admitted to hospital with a psychotic illness.

He went on to describe his relationship with his father who had been absent since John was 8 years old. John recalled his father often physically kicking him. He had an image of fighting off his father, by pushing sticks through the letterbox. After his father left home, he remarried. Subsequently, at the age of 16, John met his father in a pub with his new wife. Although John tried to dislike this woman, he found her genuine and felt that his father was now more settled. John described his mother as crazy. She had always had lots of tablets around when John was younger, and he would play with them, building towers and other constructions. His mother made a pact with him that they would both kill themselves with these tablets if things got too difficult.

On one occasion, John had talked about being bullied in school to a teacher who seemed interested in helping him. This led on, some time later, to the teacher visiting John in his own house. Later, the teacher brought John to live with him and became his guardian.

Following my assessment, and a separate nursing assessment, John was admitted to the Adolescent Unit at the Cassel Hospital for a period of inpatient assessment and possible ongoing treatment. From the initial assessment it was felt that John might be overwhelmed by the intensity of inpatient treatment and feel trapped in a world experienced as maddening. He was offered the option of starting as a day patient, coming in for two days a week. However, this setting stirred up in him feelings of being an outsider, not any more part of home and not yet part of the group of patients at the Cassel. It increased his anxiety of not being held in mind properly and brought up a lot of painful memories about the insecurity of his childhood.

On becoming an inpatient, John's anxieties immediately changed. His need for his own space, which should not be intruded upon, was apparent. He felt invaded by the distress of other patients, particularly if he could not understand what was going on for them. He felt the need to help but could not bear to be with his fellow patients. Often, for the first month, he would leave the hospital to go home to his guardian. This relieved his anxiety but, however, left him quite guilty and hopeless about his capacity to change.

In his individual sessions John was, from the beginning, invaded by memories and feelings of an unbearable intensity, without having any control. For a long time he would only come to every second session. He easily felt intruded into by what was said, and interpretations triggered off very painful memories of his past, during which he was subjected to abuse and negligence. In spite of the difficulties John faced during treatment, he could from the very beginning experience and maintain a wish to be helped, and, as therapy went on, he was very grateful for the help he got.

After a few months his sexuality became a big issue. He increasingly opened up and expressed his doubt about whether he could ever have a satisfactory, non-abusive relationship with a woman. This was a particularly difficult time in his therapy as he was terrified that any wish to come to a session was contaminated with sexual feelings. He was very sensitive to the issue of boundaries, and it gave him great relief whenever he realized that his therapist protected the therapeutic space. Maintaining boundaries was at times difficult, as John could get caught up in an excitement linked with the breaking of boundaries or the fantasy of intruding into someone else—for example, by telling his therapist things with the intention of shocking her and watching her reaction. He also communicated despair and a great need to be told that he induced warm feelings in patients and staff. This equally terrified him, as he expected something cruel and abusive hidden behind a very warm approach.

John's violent feelings became another important issue as treatment progressed. In his therapy, as well as in the inpatient therapeutic community, he would adopt a very threatening and humiliating stance, particularly if he felt intimidated. Seeing others frightened made him feel more secure. It also excited him. However, he feared being carried away by this excitement and hoped that someone could stop him. John increasingly became aware of the way he treated his objects, both internally and externally. This awareness put him in touch with his despair, and for a while he felt very hopeless about his capacity to change and repair the damage he had done. He was quite suicidal. He could, however, appreciate the help of patients and felt helped by his therapy. He began to look at issues connected with his family and to deal with the feelings this brought up. In family meetings with his guardian, he talked about his extremely difficult childhood and his guilt about leaving his mother.

During this time, John also took on a highly responsible job in the inpatient therapeutic community which involved him having a lot of close contact with other patients. He was now able to carry out this responsibility in a helpful and thoughtful way, in contrast to the situation at the beginning of his treatment when he had given up this same job after a week, feeling it was too difficult.

The time shortly before and after a Christmas break, and the weeks leading up to his leaving the inpatient setting, were difficult. He treated staff, including his therapist, with contempt and could hardly acknowledge how petrified he felt about leaving. He denied this in a very angry, omnipotent way. Nevertheless, this changed as John felt more secure about the arrangements that would follow his discharge. With the support of his psychosocial nurse, he organized his return to art college. He met with the Cassel outreach nurse and also with the consultant psychotherapist responsible for his future care. This left him feeling more hopeful about continuing to be helped following discharge. John, towards the end of treatment, experienced gratitude towards staff and patients, which was felt as very important for him.

Conclusion

I have taken you on a journey through the transitory world of adolescence. There is a sparseness of psychoanalytic writing on adolescence that perhaps reflects a time that impacts hugely yet passes away into something else so quickly. This has been captured by a number of writers (Anderson & Dartington, 1998; Blos, 1979; Copeley, 1993; Laufer & Laufer, 1984). My chapter has taken us through the experiences of working, whether as a patient or as a staff member, in the Adolescent Service at the Cassel Hospital. It is a journey from the serious, playful world of childhood to the responsible work of adulthood, whether within one's career, one's family life, or one's social and leisure time. Adolescents remain connected with the fantastical world of the child while in time developing responsible attitudes towards their personal, family, work, and social lives. If we are lucky as adolescents, we will not feel forced to give up the playfulness of childhood experiences in order to take on the ongoing cares and responsibilities of the adult world. At its best, adolescence is a time of internal and external freedom within safe limits. It is a time of major development and change. It is a hugely important time in the life of an individual, but, like all time, is transitory. The world of the adolescent is a truly transitory world.

CHAPTER SEVEN

The darkling plain: the inpatient treatment of a severely disturbed borderline adolescent

Lisa Morice and Steve McCluskey

> ... Let us be true
> To one another! For the world which seems
> To lie before us like a land of dreams,
> So various, so beautiful, so new,
> Hath really neither joy, nor love, nor light,
> Nor certitude, nor peace, nor help for pain;
> And we are here as on a darkling plain,
> Swept with confused alarms of struggle and flight,
> Where ignorant armies clash by night.
>
> from "Dover Beach", by Matthew Arnold (1867)

W hen Matthew Arnold wrote "Dover Beach" in the mid-1800s, he was not, of course, talking about inpatient work with severely disturbed borderline adolescents, but this part of his poem describes the plight of nurse, therapist, and patient working together to modify the persecution of an adolescent's inner world.

Working with severely disturbed borderline adolescents brings confusion, pain, and the sense of being useless, helpless, and alone. There seems to be no way around this. In fact, if these states are avoided too much, the work is often sterile since these feelings are frequently the result of powerful communications from the "war zone" of the patient's internal world. Our hope as clinicians is to experience them, contain them, and somehow to keep thinking. In our work with the adolescent patient that we describe in this chapter, we failed at this time and again but managed to pick ourselves up, often with the help of the rest of the Adolescent Unit team, and struggle on, remaining "true to one another".

The nursing work and the psychotherapy with this patient, Rachel, are discussed, and while there are many differences in the role of the nurse and therapist and our working relationship with the patient, several common interrelated themes emerge. We have highlighted three that seemed crucial in the work with Rachel. Firstly, the issue of emotional containment; second, the terrible distress caused by separation; and third, the difficulties of working with the concrete psychotic thinking that can be common in patients with borderline personalities.

At the end of the chapter, we also reflect upon the relationship between us as nurse and therapist and some of the dynamics that arose. This offers another way of understanding the communications of our patient.

Rachel

Rachel was born ten months after her sister Harriett, who was felt to occupy almost all of their mother's available emotional space. Rachel was filled with hatred for Harriett and also for her mother whom she described with great contempt as having been a whore, a drunk, and physically abusive to her. She told of times when her mother had beaten her. Once, she said, her mother had held her thumb in the door and slammed it; another time she had pulled her upstairs by her hair. "I used to lock myself in the downstairs cupboard to hide from her. She would stand on the other side promising that she loved me and forgave me and would not hit me any more. When I opened the door she'd pull me out and beat me again."

It should be pretty clear that, even if Rachel had exaggerated her mother's cruelty, her mother does not seem to have been capable of holding distress, making sense of it, and allowing Rachel to take in a sense of herself as lovable and understandable. Instead, Rachel took in a picture of a cruel mother with a hateful, unlovable, and bad baby who returned her mother's hatred with her own hatred.

Rachel felt that her father was the parent who loved her and raised her while her mother was taken up with her sister. Her parents separated when she was 5 years old, and Rachel felt that her mother had driven her father away because she had also beaten him. After a short while, her mother refused to allow the father contact with the girls and even implied in a court hearing that he was not their real father.

When her mother remarried, Rachel became very close to her stepfather, who, like her father, became the parent she felt really cared for her and whom she idealized. It must be said, however, that neither of these men had been able to protect Rachel from the violence of her mother and so could not be described as truly having been good for her.

Rachel was 17 when her stepfather became ill with lung cancer, from which he died a year later. When it became obvious to her how ill he was and that he would die and leave her, she left first and fled to Morocco, where she welcomed the oblivion of hard and soft drugs upon which she became heavily dependent. Her drug habit was expensive, and she became a prostitute to pay for it. This continued to some extent when she returned to England. It was both a source of triumphant pride as well as self-hatred.

Rachel lived with her boyfriend, who was a drug dealer, in a stormy and violent relationship. When they broke up she took a serious overdose. She was referred to the Cassel by the consultant psychiatrist who was alarmed by the extent of Rachel's self-destructiveness and breakdown.

Nursing on the battlefield

Psychosocial nursing at the Cassel takes place in group and individual settings and focuses on the activities of everyday life such as cooking, eating, working, and sleeping. Patients, alongside nurses, actively participate in the life of the hospital community and are encouraged to take responsibility for its everyday domestic functioning (Griffiths & Pringle, 1997). Through such tasks, the nature and meaning of the patient's relationships with others comes alive and can be explored and understood. This work provides rich material for understanding the patient's internal world. The nursing work is aimed at upholding the patient's capacity to function at a practical level and supports the strengthening of creativity and reparation (Klein, 1957). Breakdowns in the patient's relationships and functioning can also be examined and the conflicts experienced and explored. In effect, the patient's skills and pathology permeate the psychosocial nursing work.

The expectation of functioning and the taking-on of responsibilities provide support for, and the strengthening of, the patient's self-esteem, while maintaining an awareness of the need to show responsibility towards others. In the nursing arena, task and venture are shared, and this stresses for patients the possibility that help is available. It indicates that, through mutual enquiry, an individual can find some solution to his or her frustrations.

The whole essence of the psychosocial nurse's role is the use of self in the relationship with the patient—that is, the nurse uses his or her experience of being with the patient as an important therapeutic tool (Griffiths & Leach, 1997). By using the countertransference, nurses feed back the experience of what it is like to be with a patient in the service of reality testing, so that aspects of the patient's manner of relating can be understood in both their creative and their destructive elements.

Some of the work that was undertaken with Rachel about the issue of weekends, and the subsequent understanding of her states of mind before, during, and after separations, illustrates this way of working and highlights her disturbance at these times. It revealed important aspects of her destructiveness and her anxiety about her capacity for reparation, and most of all it illuminated her real struggle to tolerate feelings of guilt and concern about the damage she could do to others (Klein, 1957).

Typically, patients are expected to return to their respective homes at weekends. On the Adolescent Unit, weekends are discussed by patients and nurses, both before and after the event, in small group meetings. This forum provides the opportunity to think about weekends, the difficulties inherent in them, and the opportunity to explore how they might be managed creatively. There is a strong emphasis on helping to develop the patients' capacities to help one another, and to help draw on their own experiences and resources. In this way, patients can come to view themselves not only as people with problems but also as individuals with resources.

Early on in treatment, Rachel found this space that was provided for thinking about weekends almost intolerable. In a mocking manner she would let me know that she was delighted to be getting away from the hospital for the weekend. There were friends to see and parties to enjoy. Any attempt to reflect upon particular issues and difficulties at the time and to think about how these might encroach upon her weekends, in effect to show concern for her, were wildly dismissed. I often experienced her as pushing my concern away. She would convey that, as her nurse, I was neither wanted nor needed. Over the weeks it became increasingly clear that such experiences were a powerful communication of how she could feel at a time of impending separation—that is, that she herself felt pushed out, unwanted, and uncared-for. What was also interesting was that any rapport built up over the week between us appeared to get demolished as the end of the week approached. She would behave rudely and belligerently towards me, often leaving me feeling exasperated and humiliated. In attacking me in this way, she was also letting me know how attacked she felt and how anxious she was about managing the empty space away from the hospital, a time when carers were not there for her in a concrete way.

During this period of treatment, her return to the hospital at the beginning of the week was characterized by overt avoidant behaviour. Often she did not turn up for the different patient structures and meetings in the community, and I would find myself searching for her throughout the hospital in an attempt to make contact with her and to help her re-engage. In effect, her presence was made known through her absence. Upon finding her she would be aloof and adopt an attitude of indifference towards me, pushing me aside and, in the process, quite literally leaving me standing alone. Other patients in the hospital would quickly become enraged with her rejection of them and in turn would reject her. What got illustrated in such scenarios were the powerful feelings Rachel was able to invoke in those around her. These conflicts that she herself experienced made themselves apparent in an explicit and observable way through her relationships within the hospital. As her nurse, I used to anticipate her return with dread. This was an important indicator of what went on in her own inner world. She clearly found the loss of care at weekends humiliating, and this in turn mobilized great feelings of hatred. Her elusiveness upon her return to the hospital, coupled with a clear wish to be found, suggested to me her anxiety about being helpless and abandoned and her dread that somehow care had been destroyed. This was to be a theme throughout the course of treatment.

Amid the work with this patient about weekends, what became important to bear in mind was the fact that she did manage to return. There was, over time, an increasing sense of her ability to think with me about her painful states of mind and to perceive how these got enacted in her relationship with me and other people. She became more able to realize that such conflicts and feelings actually belonged to her. This enabled her to reach the stage where feelings about the weekend could be anticipated, together with a realization of how these feelings in turn could potentially shape her behaviour. For me, this represented her shift from excessively evacuating painful feelings into others to being a little more able to find a space inside herself for such feelings. She was able to hold on to the feelings and give them thought.

An interesting phase of treatment followed. This was a period marked, not by belligerence and hostility towards me, though this was still around, but by her allowing me to care for her and show concern. She had recently taken on a job within the hospital as an elected Adolescent Unit representative. Each of the Units within the hospital has a chairperson or persons who are responsible not only for chairing meetings, but for keeping in mind and thinking about the welfare of the patient population alongside staff teams. In this way, they help generate thoughts and solutions to problems that arise within the everyday life of the hospital community. As well as gaining from the experience of the job itself, patients

learn from the relationships they form in this role, and this en-
hances their capacity for nurturing. This was to be an important
job for Rachel, who enjoyed being able to contribute and give as
well as to receive.

What also shifted, however, was Rachel's capacity to show
some concern for herself. She started to use weekend meetings
more thoughtfully and talked about the emptiness and loneliness
that she experienced at home away from the hospital. This was a
painful part of treatment, and we heard much more about her
genuine experiences at weekends—her sense of despair, her hopelessness, and her neglect of herself. She described staying in bed
for whole weekends and eating very little. This gave a sense of the
breakdown in her ability to care for herself on her own. She was
not yet able to take the care that she experienced and received at
the Cassel home with her. This repeated breaking down was an
accurate way of showing us that she could not hold on to the
mental picture of being cared for on her own. It simply evaporated
with the separation.

At this point in treatment, Rachel had begun to reflect upon
some of her behaviours in the past, in particular her drug taking
and prostitution. Over the weeks, any thoughts about this fluctu-
ated from anxious concern to self-loathing and disgust. The pattern of how she left and returned to treatment over the weekend
period changed also. She began to leave treatment early and
return late, sometimes not returning at all, without negotiation.
An important boundary was being eroded here, and, as I began to
tackle this issue with her, the nature of her disturbance became
accessible. By leaving treatment early and returning late, I was the
one who had the experience of what it felt like to be left behind.
This communication was clear enough. She was eventually able to
reflect that her comings and goings in the manner described were
a way of having some control over feelings of loss. In an angry
outburst in one meeting, she revealed that she often spent her
weekends getting high on drugs and selling herself for sex.

This was to become an issue that was explored for some
months in the context of weekends. Rachel's getting high was a
way of escaping the emptiness and sad feelings that were aroused
in her at weekends, albeit a temporary and false measure. Her

sexual behaviour also seemed powerfully linked to feelings of loss and the disturbance aroused by the experience of separation. In one sense, she felt that by selling herself for sex she could maintain the idea that somebody was interested in her. It seemed that her desperate search for comfort, contact, and love negated her feelings of despair and isolation. Sex, quite literally, was a way of filling up the emptiness inside. However, such behaviour at weekends also allowed me to see how Rachel dealt with her feelings of rage at being left. Her contact with men in this context was a sneering and triumphant one. Relationships of this kind were about denigration and contempt. It was a performance of mockery over the idea of love and affection and companionship. It was also clearly a projection into these men of her sense of being denigrated.

What were of the utmost importance were the ongoing relationships that Rachel had within the hospital, with both staff and patients alike. What was helpful for her over time was the persistent concern over her self-abusive behaviour. Through the setting of boundaries and limits that, in essence, were an explicit statement that her self-abuse was not acceptable, she was able to experience a genuine concern of others towards her and slowly to adopt a similar attitude of concern towards herself.

Stopping such behaviours, however, presented Rachel with an enormous task. It meant that she had to face the risk of managing weekends, and the powerful feelings that got stirred up at such times, rather differently. She was faced with the reality of her destructiveness and how this, by its very nature, could wipe out any idea of care. For her, separation and loss were experienced more concretely as death, this being intimately connected with her own aggression. Faced with these issues, she was clearly anxious about how relationships could be preserved.

In a review of her treatment at the halfway point, what became clear to us as a team was Rachel's need to experience some capacity for reparation, to have a sense not only of her destructiveness but also of her creativity. This is where the true essence of the nursing work and the wider activity of the therapeutic community made its impact on her treatment. Rachel was encouraged and supported to take on a job within the hospital which involved managing an annual fund-raising event for the hospital. She poured weeks and weeks of concentrated effort into this job, which she managed very successfully. This job inspired a wide range of networks and relationships within the hospital which she experienced as very containing. She was connected to real relationships while pursuing something creative. Through this work she was able to gain more of a sense of her ability to repair what she had felt she had destroyed.

As well as helping her with this job, my work with her continued to focus on the practicalities of weekends. She was able to plan her weekends with me, structuring them in a way that provided more containment. It meant shopping and cooking for herself, visiting friends that were helpful companions, and exploring ordinary means of obtaining pleasure. There was more of a sense of Rachel making space for herself, outside the hospital, in which she could live and where nurturing could be experienced.

Holding the baby

In order to understand more clearly the foundations of communication in psychoanalytic terms, we need to look at the very early processes of projection and introjection that go on between mother and infant in the beginning of life. Melanie Klein (1946) originally developed the idea that one person could unconsciously project unwanted states of mind, or parts of the self, into another who then might actually experience them.

Bion (1962a) developed further Klein's ideas about projective identification and described the crucial importance of the mother's capacity to receive emotionally the anxious and distressed states of mind of her infant and to do what was necessary to relieve them. Bion (1962b) saw these processes of primitive communication between infant and mother, or primary caretaker, as crucial to the development of the child's capacity to think. Margot Waddell (1998) makes the point that introjection and projection are analogous to taking in what is felt to be good and healthy and expelling what is felt to be harmful or bad. As the baby's world is initially experienced via his or her relationship with the mother, he is sensitively attuned to her moods. If she laughs, the baby will smile; if the mother is upset, the baby may frown or cry. Waddell writes:

> When a baby is angry, he is totally angry with his whole being, he perceives his mother as the source of his pain and anger. Her feels bad. He wants to get rid of this feeling. He thrusts it back into the supposed source, namely his mother. In his eyes his mother herself then becomes bad, and so he takes back in the sense of having a bad mother. He has a bad mother within him. When she comforts and feeds him, and he has a good feeling, his mother again becomes good. He "projects" his bad feeling and identifies her with it. He "introjects" his experience of her as calm, satisfying and good, and he himself acquires a good feeling within. He feels himself to be "good". [Waddell, 1998, p. 213]

Waddell goes on to say that:

> When an infant's cry or smile goes without any answering echo in the mother, if she cannot respond to him emotionally, there will be no opportunity for the baby to take back in an experience of having painful feelings understood and held in a mind, or by an emotional presence, that is felt to have the care and the capacity to make things bearable for him. The bad "something" that is felt will be taken back in. [Waddell, 1998, p. 215]

In order for the baby to feel calm, this feeling will have to be reprojected in an attempt to get rid of it. If this happens too much, the baby will begin to identify herself as not understandable, as bad, and as someone who forces bad things into others.

How many times have you seen some version of the following situation? A small child falls down and hurts itself. The child starts to wail in distress. The adult looks briefly and says, "It's perfectly all right, now stop crying, hush, don't be such a baby." The child cries louder. Or, the adult might bend down to examine the hurt knee, saying something like, "Ouch, poor knee, it really hurts doesn't it", and maybe offers the child a hug or kiss. The child stops crying. In the second situation the child's distress has been received and contained by the adult, and so the child feels better. In the first situation, the distress is not received, so the bad feeling is worse and the child tries harder to "put it into" the adult for containment.

Before going on to describe the psychotherapeutic work with Rachel more fully, the following brief clinical material should illustrate the rough end of this concept as I experienced it in my countertransference to Rachel (Heimann, 1950). Rachel had always complained that the time of her 8.00 a.m. Tuesday session was too early and often demanded that I change it. Fran was another patient of mine with whom Rachel felt terribly rivalrous and who had a later time in the morning. Normally, upon coming into the hospital, clinical staff read the nurse's summaries of the shifts during their absences. On this particular morning, I came in just before the session with Rachel and had not read reports of the night shift before she arrived to see me. Before I had a chance to get properly seated, Rachel leaned forward and said "Well, Fran's gone, I want her session." I said that I did not understand what she meant. She said very impatiently, "I said, Fran's gone and I want her time—mine is too early." Again I said I did not know what she meant by Fran being gone. She shouted, "She's hung herself, she's gone, now give me her time!" I felt appalled, unable to think, and said "What?" She said, with a note of airy contempt, "Oh she didn't die, I thought you knew, she's gone to another hospital, so now I want her time." After a struggle, I managed to say that maybe we were meant to quickly think of changing the session time in order not to think of the awfulness of what had happened.

At this point, Rachel went into a tirade of blaming me and the staff for Fran's attempt to hang herself and thereby passed over to me all the unbearable guilt and the sense of persecution and terror that her hatred of Fran, and her nastiness towards her, had caused. I was left not only with my own sense of guilt and horror, but all of Rachel's. I could barely move after she left.

Surviving concrete thinking

Important aspects of Rachel's borderline functioning and treatment were her concrete thinking, which at times was psychotic, and her great difficulty with separations. This included her inability to keep good and bad separate in her mind, which was in a terrible muddle, as well as her difficulty separating from me at the end of sessions and on weekends and holidays. For these kinds of patients, the separation from the therapist, or any helping person to whom they are attached, is experienced as a brutal rejection and a cruel abandonment. In these cases, the loss is felt to be final and irreversible. In order to protect herself from this terrible pain, Rachel had to destroy quickly her own sense of hope in my concern for her as her therapist and her dependence on me to help her, which might have been gained from session to session. In this way, she tried not to feel vulnerable to loss. The end of the week, when our patients return home, was particularly difficult for her to bear. I was the one who had to be made to feel the destruction of my hopes for her, a sense of being utterly thrown out and being made to experience an attack on my professional abilities that often added up to a sense of my complete worthlessness. Often I felt that the best I could do was survive.

When I talk about survival here, I am going beyond the concept of my survival as a thinking therapist and into the arena of my actual physical survival in Rachel's mind. For instance, after one Thursday session in which she had been particularly brutal to me, she worried the whole weekend that I had been so devastated that I would actually kill myself. Her difficulty distinguishing fantasy from reality meant that she was often convinced that her murderous wishes could really kill. This was very persecuting for her. She was desperate to feel that I could protect myself and that the staff could protect other patients from her murderous wishes—much in the same way that she had needed her father and stepfather to protect her as a child from the murderousness of her mother. Not only was it terribly important to her that I survived her attacks, but that on my return I could keep thinking with her about her distress rather than punish her. In this way, bit by bit, I think she began to feel that her unbearable feelings could be borne. In the following case material I hope to show both her concrete thinking and the problem this raised for me in finding a way to talk with her.

In one session, Rachel eloquently described her inability to believe that she had a real separate identity of her own. She told me that she did not really ever know what was true about herself. She tried to figure it out and remember the way things really were, but her mother's voice in her mind told her something else and she ended up not knowing again. She tried to think of herself as an okay person, but her mother's voice told her she was not. At times she also felt that she *was* her mother.

I said it was difficult for her to think that there were ways she might be like her mother instead of being her mother. In response she said: "But I feel like I *am* my mother all the time—not just like her but that she is actually in my body. I fight this. I tell myself of course I'm not my Mum, but it goes on and on—like a battle in my mind. It scares me, it sounds schizophrenic, it's mad. I don't know who I am."

During the next few sessions, she went on with this theme. It was very difficult for me to find a way to talk to her about it because of her concreteness. Her state of mind was often her state of body. If I explored with her this "mother's voice" in her mind, she began to feel more and more that I was believing with her that her mother actually existed inside her. In one session she came in and said: "I'm really angry with you today for making me feel so dirty—with my mum inside of me. I want to scrape off all my skin but she'd be the bones inside me—she'd like that."

Two days later she took an overdose of thirty-eight Paracetamol, which, she told me, was to kill off the mother inside her. I think she was telling me that I had failed, like her stepfather, to protect her from her murderous mother, so she was left to do the job herself. It was only when I could take up strenuously the differences between her and her mother that she could calm down.

I said that she had told me of ways she was *different* from her mother, that she *knew* it was wrong to treat a little child the way she had been treated by her mother, and I listed some of the things she had described that she knew were wrong. I went on to say that she had come for treatment because she did not want to be that way herself but to strengthen the part of her that was different and knew it was not right. To the extent that I could do this, I felt that I could be of real help. From that point on, however, I had to deal with my growing anxiety about finding a way of talking with her that would not cause more damage, or even cause her death.

Surviving hatred

The following clinical material illustrates Rachel's terrible confusion between what was good for her and what was bad, including whether I, as her therapist, was good for her or bad (Klein, 1957). The material also illustrates her inability to manage separations from me. Breaks in therapy for weekends and holidays further increased her muddle about my goodness or badness.

In one session, she described her mind as a jumbled up pile of Coca-Cola and Pepsi cans. She said they were all mixed up, and she wished she could get them separated into the good Coke cans in one pile and the bad Pepsi cans in another, with strings that could connect them. She said she liked Coke and not Pepsi. I think this was a perfect description of her difficulty with establishing a proper split between good and bad. If one thinks for a minute about Coke and Pepsi, there is probably not much difference between them except their flavour and neither could be said to be nourishing. Also, Rachel had snorted a lot of cocaine in her day, so I had my doubts about this "good" Coke. It was a though she was trying to make a good and bad thing out of two things that were not really good for her. There were times when her mother had seemed good and loving, only to turn quickly cruel again. Her father and stepfather were also muddled in her mind in terms of good and bad. On the one hand, both were seen to be kind and caring in so many ways, but, on the other, in wanting "a quiet life" they did not stand up to her mother and say, "No, this is a bad way to treat a child and you cannot do it!"

Her relationship with me was also muddled in this way. Not only ends of sessions, weekends, and holiday breaks, but any lapse in my attention or withholding of instant relief from her distress were ample reasons for her to feel that I did not care about her and to attack me. "You don't give a damn about me", she would say: "You care more about your hair and your clothes. You go off to your cushy little life and leave me here with all these crazy people. You are useless, you haven't helped me at all. They must have made a mistake and sent you the wrong letter when they hired you." She would often stamp out of the room five minutes before the end of the session, slamming the door and shouting down the hall, "Stick your sessions up your ass and fuck you Mrs Morice." This is a fairly graphic example of her putting the badness into me at the point of separation.

Sometimes it was almost worse when she believed, for a few moments, even most of a session, that I might really be concerned about her. When she became aware of the approaching end, she would say, "You're tricking me, you're just pretending to be nice, leave me alone!" She would rush away, leaving me once again with my crumbled hopes for the survival of a good contact between us. As she had to protect herself from loss by attacking me and our bits of good work, it made it painfully difficult for her to keep anything good or alive inside herself from the sessions to help her through the breaks. Again and again I was the one who had to bear or contain the feelings of being useless and thrown away and, at the same time, to keep some hope for her alive.

Her conviction that I was only interested in fattening up my own ego on her dependence and distress reminds me of the fairy tale of Hansel and Gretel. I was like the wicked witch who lures in the hungry and abandoned children with promises of lovely food and warmth, but whose real intent is to fatten them up for the kill and to devour them. It was sometimes possible to present this dilemma to her in the middle of sessions, but rarely at the end.

Another aspect of this dynamic was that she was also sure that, in addition to feeding my own ego, I was offering real concern and help to others. In the inpatient setting, she felt that my other patients were the favoured sisters and she often was a cruel bully towards them. When Fran attempted to hang herself, it left Rachel feeling that she could triumphantly occupy both her session time and her place in my mind and my affections. However, it also left her open to persecution from her terrible sense of guilt for having felt that she had almost concretely killed off one of her rivals.

Very gradually she began to think that it might just be possible to repair some of the damage that she felt she caused and to stop the internal warfare with her mother and her external warfare with me. In the beginning of this phase, these attempts were desperate, manic, and sounded quite crazy, but they contained her wish to put things right that she felt she had destroyed.

Just before my return from my Easter holiday, Rachel had visited her stepfather's grave with her nurse. She came to her first session with me a few minutes early, and in the company of a nurse. I think she had been frightened to find that I might be dead, especially given the fury of her angry attacks against me before my holiday. She was left during the break struggling to keep stepfather and me alive in her mind in the face of her rage. She asked me: "Did you have a good holiday, Mrs Morice? I'm waiting for my dad to come—he's coming to see me now. See, I'm wearing his shirt and here's his picture. The room looks different—you look different—your hair is permed, it looks really nice that way. I missed you when you were gone. I didn't think I would, but I really did. It surprised me, but I guess I must like you more than I thought—but you weren't here—I was quite sad really. You weren't here when I needed you. I felt so sad. I'm waiting for my dad to come now and I'll give him a really good dinner." Then she noticed that there was no coat on my hanger, and she asked, "Are you cold Mrs Morice? I'll go and get you a coat." I said she wanted to be sure I was all right. Rachel agreed, and I went on to say that she was trying so hard to take care of me like she wished she could take care of her dad, and that she was trying also to protect me from how angry she was that I had been away.

She agreed again and said, "I won't be mean to you any more, I won't say I want another therapist—you're fine." Technically, I felt it was important here to support the effort she was making to be on the side of protection and repair, rather than point out her mania and her split-off destructive wishes.

Little by little, Rachel began to establish the beginning of real separation between what was good for her and what was bad. She began to care for herself properly at weekends, as described in the nursing work. This progress was very tentative and subject to constant setbacks, but it went on.

As also described in the nursing work, the pressure of my summer holiday, along with her nurse's, was terrible for Rachel, but the thing that I believe was impossible for her to bear was her own imminent departure from the hospital two months later. I think she experienced this as being thrown away and left, a sort of death of our concern and care for her. As she did when her stepfather was dying, she left the Cassel a month early in an attempt to be the one in charge of the loss. It was the only way she could manage, and this had to be respected. In our last session she said, "If I stay here now, Mrs Morice, it will kill me."

On follow-up, her ability to manage painful or depressed feelings was still very shaky, and often she fell back on the use of drugs to cope. Unfortunately, these drugs brought on bouts of psychosis. However, her new boyfriend of several months was a far more caring person than others had been, and he tried very hard to keep her healthy and to stop Rachel from abusing her body. Likewise, she had begun to choose friends who promoted things that were good for her, unlike the last group, who had been intent on drugs and promiscuous sex. It did seem that at least she knew what was good for her even though she could not always act on this knowledge.

This was something of the nature of the struggle that Rachel and I had together. I was made to feel useless, worthless, and was given the "sack" at the end of most sessions. It was my sense that I had to feel these things for Rachel who found them too difficult. This illustrates also her difficulty in distinguishing reality from phantasy, her inability to tell good from bad, and her inability to believe that I could care about her between sessions and keep a space for her in my mind free of other patients. Her destructive attacks on me and our work together were not only a way of protecting herself from her feelings of vulnerability and abandonment, but a way of communicating to me the real pain of those feelings.

Long-term follow-up, after several years, found Rachel married to a man who was very concerned about her well-being. She had stopped all use of street drugs, and her psychotic episodes were infrequent and were managed with medication prescribed by her consultant psychiatrist. Rachel was working in a job that she liked and seemed hopeful about her future. Often we find that the distress of leaving the Cassel after a year's intensive treatment is so painful that it can be some time before the benefits are apparent.

Help from our friends

We have tried to show that working closely with patients with borderline personalities—or, indeed, any distressed adolescent— can be an enormous strain. Workers have to sustain themselves in the face of powerful and disturbing communications. This often means that very painful feelings have to be experienced and contained while preserving the capacity to think. Often these feelings came alive in the nurse–therapist couple as well as in the Adolescent Unit team.

A frequent phenomenon in our work is that one worker will be seen as the good, understanding one, and another will be seen as the useless, stupid one who never gets it right. With Rachel, it was sometimes her nurse who was felt to be this "good" worker, and her therapist who was seen as the cruel, rejecting one. Often this switched around. It is very pleasant to be on the good side of a split, and sometimes we both found ourselves seduced by it, thinking the other to be a bit insensitive and not understanding the best way of helping Rachel.

This kind of splitting was also found in divisions between the inpatient staff, who sometimes saw themselves as the ones who really understood, and the outpatient workers, who often thought that we were out of touch and did not understand the real problems facing Rachel. At some point this splitting must be understood as a way the patient survives—by ejecting the "bad" bits of themselves into some member of the network and identifying that person as bad. If other members go along with this and try to remain "good", leaving fellow workers to be "bad", it can cause a lot of problems. There were frequent times when nurse and therapist each felt a conviction that his or her own work was useless and that the "real work" was being done by the other who was having all the good therapeutic interactions with Rachel. In nurse–therapist supervisions, it was possible to pick this up between us and thus keep a harboured resentment from growing up. It helped us to understand Rachel in an emotionally immediate way. During this time, we had each been feeling ourselves to be the "bad" worker; we found that each of us had been experiencing Rachel's own conviction that the apparently rich resources of her workers were going to someone else and that she was herself empty and useless. This was the same painful feeling Rachel had about her sister Harriett having all the best of their mother. This terrible feeling had been got rid of into us in a way that we actually experienced this.

Frequent team meetings also helped with this and kept us, as nurse and therapist, in touch with the other's experience as well as with the experiences of the rest of the team. This is vitally important, not only for the emotional support necessary to keep going, but also to be on the lookout for these kinds of enactments of our patient's difficult and projected feelings.

Conclusion

We have tried to give the emotional flavour of the work with this young woman as well as to describe aspects of the psychosocial nursing work and the work in individual psychotherapy. The aspects we described were our attempt to provide emotional containment, the severe difficulty of working with separations during her treatment, and the struggles to work safely with her concrete thinking. We have described also the importance of maintaining the link between the two workers and the difficulties involved because of the splitting that is inevitable in this work.

CHAPTER EIGHT

The containment
of borderline adolescents

Denis Flynn and Joanne Turner

To that truth which has the look of falsehood
A man should always close his lips, if he can . . .

Dante, *The Divine Comedy*; Inferno, Canto XVI, 124

In this chapter we look at the containment of borderline adolescents as they begin or undergo treatment in a therapeutic-community setting. Importantly, this containment includes the complex task of understanding the meaning of the adolescent's symptoms and his or her mental states and social behaviour. The patients concerned belong, in the main, to the middle and severe end of the borderline personality disorder spectrum. Some of these patients have, from time to time or in the past, experienced some psychotic symptoms or episodes, along with major self-harm, severe depression, psychosomatic complaints, and suicide attempts, and they may, like many disturbed adolescents, fear the occurrence of a major psychotic breakdown.

The context of treatment is the Adolescent Unit at the Cassel Hospital, which is part of a therapeutic community with intensive psychosocial nursing and a significant input of psychoanalytic psychotherapy, where the relationships and attachments that develop become the subject of enquiry and the focus of personal growth and change.

There are particular problems of containment for borderline adolescents, who may undergo temporary psychotic or delusional states. We begin this chapter by describing the context or setting of therapeutic treatment, in particular from a nursing perspective. The focus is on the minimal and maximal conditions where learning and change can take place. Next, we sketch out some psychoanalytic ideas about borderline psychotic conditions and their relevance to the treatment of adolescents. There then follows some composite treatment examples of individual adolescents.

At the outset we would like to stress that we are not claiming that the therapeutic community can successfully treat borderline adolescents who experience psychotic states for prolonged periods. We do hope to show, however, that some adolescents who have or have had temporary psychotic episodes can, in some circumstances, be contained in a therapeutic-community setting, so that their treatment can proceed, without collapse or breakdown, and further improvements can be made. Others, however, cannot be so contained and need to transfer to an acute unit and be treated by medication and continuous observation.

When treating the very disturbed adolescent, the diagnosis, our knowledge of the history and aetiology of his or her problems, and our views and reactions may change as the adolescent changes. It is important, then, to have a treatment modality that is sensitive both to the overall general development of adolescents and to severe forms of adolescent disturbance and behaviour, including possible incipient forms of psychosis. We believe that it is important to hold on to the idea that therapeutic forms of treatment and management for highly disturbed adolescents may offer something useful at different points in their development and at different stages of their disturbance.

We shall look at these issues from both an individual and a group perspective, that of the therapeutic community. A shift of thinking took place when Bion, Tom Main, Maxwell Jones, and others developed the idea that neurosis was not simply an individual problem, but was a problem of the group. As Bion and Rickman put it in the first therapeutic-community experiment, at the Northfield hospital during the Second World War, "Neurosis needs to be displayed as a danger to the group; and its display must somehow be made the common aim of the group" (Bion, 1961, pp. 13–14). Within life in institutions, neurosis becomes manifest and is experienced in the group as an interference to group functioning, or, in Bion's later terms, to the "work group". When this happens, individuals can take responsibility, as can members of the group as a whole, to become "self-critical" (p. 18) and then to undertake work to change the group functioning. Bion's and Main's further work uncovered the underlying psychotic processes in individual and group behaviour (Bion, 1962b; Main, 1957). We now understand that, particularly with borderline patients, severe disturbance becomes manifest in disturbed group and institutionalized functioning. Our treatment structures in the Adolescent Unit have developed to address such disturbance and have lead to new areas of understanding, especially about the requirements of staff responses in managing these processes.

The context of therapeutic treatment

Normally, young people of both sexes, aged 16 to 21 years, come for up to a year's treatment in the inpatient Adolescent Unit at the Cassel Hospital. There are different elements of the treatment, under the separate headings of psychotherapy (twice-weekly group, twice-weekly individual, and psychosocial nursing in the therapeutic community. The psychotherapy looks at the inner world, phantasies, and the transference. In the applied inpatient setting, this means not just individual transferences to psychotherapist or nurse, or other staff members, but also group or split transferences and transferences to the institution. The work of the nurses centrally involves development of an understanding of the emotional meaning of behaviour and the impact of real events, during both day and night, and the development of relationships and attachments. Both these aspects of treatment are seen to be in the psychoanalytic sense "mutative"—that is, they can lead to lasting psychic change. The complex processes of this treatment, and the stresses on individuals and groups, need to be understood in daily staff meetings, ongoing reviews, nurse–therapist supervisions, a whole-hospital "strains" meeting, and so on. The "strains" meeting looks at and thinks about the feelings and mood of the staff, including their morale, important institutional issues that they face as staff, plus influences on them from patients— their countertransference in their work and possible unconscious enactments by staff, individually or collectively. The place given to structures to help the staff be contained, and to think about and process what they are doing, is one of the most important aspects of the therapeutic programme.

Patients have an active part in treatment. They organize all aspects of the daily living, including rooms, meals (except the midday meal), and activities and events within the hospital. Equally importantly they organize unit and community meetings, as well as a whole host of other meetings in the day and evenings, to look at emotional issues arising for individuals and the group, and they devise helping methods to deal with them. At night there is only one clinical member of staff at the hospital, the duty nurse, and the patients' first point of call is a night orderly. There is, of course, a back-up duty team outside the hospital, but most ongoing issues are dealt with by the patients, with the involvement of the night nurse. Practical solutions about how patients manage are discussed and applied, using what understanding is available. Issues that arise from these crises and attempts to manage can be brought back into the day for consideration within nursing structures and in psychotherapy. In an everyday way, the patients deal with the impact of disturbance—their own and that of other patients—on each other, and share responsibility at looking at it. One of the major factors that determines whether the patient has the capacity and the support to stay in this form of treatment is whether they are forming relationships with other patients and whether they are accepted by those patients. Most often it is the relationships that adolescents have with others that provide the most powerful affective emotional component in treatment. We think the reason for this—something we shall explore in the examples below—is that hidden disturbed elements, including psychotic projections, become entwined in the culture of the adolescent group and the hospital as an institution. We assess, therefore, not just individual progress in psychotherapy and in the nursing work, but the impact of the adolescent on the community and, vice-versa, the impact of the community on the adolescent. In doing this, we assess the culture of the adolescent group within the therapeutic community.

The central message or philosophy is that the patients can contain themselves with help and support from each other and from staff. The emphasis is on their functioning and strength rather than their collapse. There are various roles and jobs that patients can take on and work at, which increases the amount of contact and discussion or support they get from staff members. This live ongoing contact with their nurse supports functioning and helps in the understanding of emerging disturbance. It is the relationships that the adolescents form in various settings that are containing.

To guide these relationships, there are three clear boundaries for patients about acceptable behaviour, which we attempt to apply consistently. These are: no alcohol or street drugs, no violence, and no sexual relationships. These are clear, minimal, and straightforward and have been the subject of discussion by the "community management team". This consists of patients and staff who meet weekly to discuss and decide on issues affecting the whole community. Hopefully this means that the rules are owned by the community of patients, and it increases the likelihood that they will be adhered to. Obviously rules get broken. Particularly with adolescents the rules get "tested", and therefore there are some sanctions to deal with this. If all attempts to work with and collaborate with a person have failed, and there is no agreement about being in treatment, ultimately they may be discharged. This provision is the cause of considerable anger to patients, and of envy to workers in other services, who often cannot require the patient to agree to treatment. However, the measure most frequently used is "short leave". This is time out for both the individual concerned and the community and the staff, and a time to think about the effect of the behaviour, the reasons for it, and how it can be different. Usually, once a boundary has been re-established by saying "No" to certain behaviour, patients can resume treatment and can often move on. At the end of short leave, there will be a "management meeting", normally with the senior nurse and consultant, to discuss with the patient an under-standing of what was happening and how this may make treat-ment different.

> Judy is an 18-year-old girl with a history of sexual abuse by her stepfather. Following his prosecution and imprisonment for this offence, Judy was totally rejected by her family. On the day of the court verdict, she had been given half an hour to grab her belongings and leave the family home. She began to self-harm severely by burning and cutting, eventually needing several skin grafts. She lived in an adolescent unit for two years and had been allowed to stay much longer than anybody before her. She then moved to a social services hostel in preparation for her admission to the Cassel. She had established friendly relationships with professionals that included inappropriately meeting up at weekends or spending holiday time together. There was a huge effort to understand Judy's self-harm and be sympathetic to its causes. Although she was given a lot of help to stop the self-harm, this did not happen, and the self-harm got much worse. She was becoming, in Main's sense in "The Ailment" (1957), a "special patient".

She was met prior to her admission to the Cassel by the senior nurse and consultant to start to establish some boundaries, clearest of which was the requirement to curb severe self-harm. Otherwise we would not be able to work with her. She had attended this meeting on crutches after having had a skin graft on her leg, due to another serious episode of self-harm. She was so furious with this meeting, feeling we did not under-stand her, that she turned down admission. The already lengthy assessment was put on hold. Several months later, however, after another admission to hospital for self-harm, she wrote to ask to be reconsidered and was then reassessed and subsequently admitted.

During her six-week assessment, she mostly kept herself safe but remote, and there was just one incident of superficial burning during this time. Judy remained obsessed by self-harm and yet always presented herself as struggling with it, so that in fact it was extremely hard to get to know her. Then her therapist went on holiday, leaving her with her male nurse. Judy went on weekend leave early, saying there was nothing at the hospital for her. At the end of the therapist's holiday, when it was becoming clear that Judy felt abandoned and envious of the family she assumed her therapist to have, she lacerated her wrists and needed surgery to repair the damage.

Judy then missed the first session she was to have had on her therapist's return from leave. In the usual morning meeting between nurses and patients, Judy claimed there was no connection between her self-harm and her therapist's holiday. She felt that she should be able just to continue as she was at the hospital and gave a bland, perfunctory understanding of why she had done what she had. She was met for a management meeting and sent on short leave. Judy was furious, and only then in her rage did she express her feelings about being disappointed and how this made her self-harm. Up until then, she had not as yet expressed this at all or in any way really attempted to work with what she felt. She just thought we should "understand" her reasons, without her owning them or struggling with change. There was a ring of falsity about this and an appeal from injured narcissism. (We refer you to the quote from Dante at the beginning of the chapter and to Freud, 1914c.)

Judy was outraged, then, that she would be sent away. When she returned after a week away, however, she was much more thoughtful, more open about her anger, more willing to express it, and more realistic about what she needed to do in treatment. It was the last time she self-harmed in her treatment, and she has since looked upon this management meeting as a turning point in her growth towards health and independence. Our use of the sanction of "short leave" in this situation underlined our view that her self-harm was perpetuated by her unthinking and other's collusive acceptance of her destructive and narcissistic behaviour, which prevented the development of other, more ordinary and sane attachments. We shall return to this theme again below.

In crisis situations, patients are expected to help with the management of other patients and have opinions on what may best help. This includes taking on responsibility for supervision of individuals who are especially vulnerable or at risk in planned arrangements with other patients or alongside staff members. Medication is not given as a quick fix. Most adolescent patients dispense with psychotropic medication before or during treatment. We expect patients to ask each other for help—that is, to spend time with them, talk to them, or involve them in activities. Individual patients who are themselves in crisis are expected to make a plan for themselves with others' help, and to be involved in saying what they need for that particular time. In other words they are expected to be active, not passive, and to take active control in dealing with symptoms, their illness, and their progress.

Each patient has a first nurse who has his or her particular needs and treatment aims in mind. The emphasis, once again, is that this relationship is one of collaboration and of understanding about how things can be done together. Nurses organize activities with patients and think with them about the practical tasks of the day and how their relationships with others affect these. They are expected to use their feelings to feed back and reflect on what the patient may be experiencing. Therefore, the process of doing a task is as important as the end result.

> Maureen is a 20-year-old borderline patient, who had suffered severe paranoid delusions of a psychotic nature, leading to confused mental states and severe self-harm. Several severe episodes involved a type of splitting that was such that the disturbance showed itself outside the hospital or in relation to the boundaries of treatment, particularly in her threats of violence (described in detail later). We struggled continually with Maureen to get her to express her experiences of relationships and tasks on the unit, including getting her to express her disturbance within the hospital.

> About ten months into treatment this seemed more possible at times. Maureen was habitually meticulously tidy, both at home and in her room in the hospital. She had always taken tasks at the Cassel to do with such cleaning very seriously, even when

she had been most uncooperative in other areas. She was in a work-group with her nurse, cleaning the common-room. Usually her nurse had been able to rely on her attendance. As discharge loomed, Maureen stopped attending, and she was continually having to be woken in the mornings. Her nurse began to find her behaviour infuriating. As Maureen was now not attending structures or being active in community life, the issue was discussed in a morning meeting. It became clear that Maureen was furious with staff for discharging her and was reacting in a way that she knew would be noticed and questioned—but that was nevertheless *safe*. As a serious self-harmer, this was very important. She had used the structures and the context of the morning work-group to contain her angry feelings, within treatment, rather than express them in a self-destructive way, attacking the boundaries of treatment itself.

Living in the community is perhaps the aspect of treatment that is hardest. This is because it involves twenty-four-hour living together, a troublesome sense of belonging, and the need to keep the hospital running as an ordinary place to live, with meals being planned and prepared, and activities and therapeutic structures kept going. Often the intimacy of sharing bedrooms and general living space means that the feedback and observation that patients can offer each other is crucial. The aim is always to encourage this in a constructive way, so that it is usually what other patients say that has the most impact. Patients get to know in a very immediate and real way how the behaviour, mental states, and actions of others affect them individually and as a group. The emotional impact of this is continually discussed, trawled over, and interpreted to each other. The community experience can be the first time that people feel they have belonged anywhere and the first time they realize that their feelings, behaviour, and history are not unique. They may discover that they are not alone, strange, or misfits, or, if they find that this does represent part of who they are, they may discover in interactions with others how their functioning may need to change. How they relate will affect whether there is a culture of empathy and cooperation, or a culture of antipathy, with the possibility of unresolved conflict, breakdown of social relationships, and possible chaos.

For those people who have difficult night-times, unable to settle from the day, or with nightmares and flashbacks, there is a system of night contacts. Here a patient will ask another patient to be his or her night contact so that they can then call on them during the night for support, if necessary. This works because everyone will have a time when they need to ask for help but also a time when they can offer it.

A lot of thought goes into a patient's discharge from the community, and a specific date is set at least two months in advance in order to begin the process of leaving the hospital and saying goodbye. We help to prepare young people to leave by always offering a space to talk about it and, in practical ways, with adolescents, make links with local education or set up workers' meetings to work out further therapeutic provisions following discharge. We encourage patients to attend college during their treatment and try to arrange therapy times and roles in the community that allow them to do this, provided that this is consistent with other aims in treatment.

"Adolescent function" vs. "borderline function"

Adolescence is a time of change, of unpredictable and powerful reactions and responses, with the loss of childhood and moves towards adulthood. There are powerful biological and sexual changes, a new awareness of the body, a new sense of the personal, experiences of new impulses, and an increased awareness of inner feelings and reflections. There is a shifting awareness of groups, of parents and relatives, of authority figures and institutional structures, and a wider sense of society. A normal transition through adolescence involves some measure of disturbance, both of inner feelings and attitudes—indeed, within oneself—and disturbance of others too. These processes occur in adolescence as part of a process of detachment from the parents and the family. As with earlier detachment processes in infancy, when equally there were major changes in awareness of the emotional states of others, it involves interchanging periods of integration and lack of integration, and rapid shifts between the paranoid-schizoid and depressive positions (Klein, 1932, 1946; Stern, 1985). Sometimes, adolescents—both "normal" and severely disturbed adolescents— appear static behind a wall of powerful resistances or defences, and sometimes they surge forwards in what seems a haphazard and contradictory way. The task in treating such adolescents requires an understanding that change does or can occur at any time.

We are used to the idea from psychoanalysis that it is the operation of powerful psychological mechanisms in infancy that shapes the personality, a shape that is modified but remains essentially the same at later stages of development. We think, however, that adolescence, viewed psychoanalytically, is a substantially new period of experience, growth, and change in the personality. For, underlying the changes in adolescence, just as in infancy, there are major shifts in the relation of the superego and ego to the increased id drives and continuous processes of projective identification and splitting and fragmentation of the ego, which alter the boundaries of internal and external reality and change the shape of the personality in a fundamentally new way (Flynn, 2000; A. Freud, 1936; Klein, 1932, 1946). Adolescents with borderline disturbances exemplify these changes in a particularly marked way.

Bion's (1962a) theory of containment, and of negative and positive projective identification, develops further this theory for the understanding of adolescents. Over time the adolescent learns to contain in his or her mind the thoughts and feelings that led to progressive splitting and projective identification, until he or she begins to feel that his or her own mind, and body, can contain what is going on. Throughout adolescence, and any adolescent's day, there are constant shifts backwards and forwards between disturbed and calmer periods, between paranoid–schizoid and depressive positions, Ps↔D, as Bion described it. In understanding the adolescent, one needs to allow an experience of the feelings and thoughts of the adolescent in their split and fragmented state, in the paranoid position. Over time this receptive capacity—the containment in the mind of the analyst/therapist/parent of such disturbed and fragmented elements—allows for something different to develop, and some pattern emerges in the depressive position. The adolescent, aware of this process of containment, internalizes at certain points this good figure. The adolescent then uses this internalized receptive capacity him/herself and develops more reflective and depressive capacities. It is in this sort of process that the adolescent builds up a new inner (internal) world. We are all familiar with the situation of the adolescent, or parent, stuck in the paranoid-schizoid position, feeling isolated, misunderstood, literally paranoid and torn apart. Importantly, too, the adolescent learns more fully *a sense of value*, not simply in the Freudian sense, but in a new sense of a sexual body and worked-through oedipal relations and a capacity to contain him/herself. Our experience in working with the most severely disturbed adolescents is that the attainment of this sense of value is the single most important objective in adolescence. In normal adolescence, after attaining to some degree this sense of emotional value, the tasks of adulthood can begin to be faced.

In pathological adolescent disturbance, there is what Klein and Bion call "excessive projective identification", a continued confusion and distortion of internal and external reality. Such adolescent disturbance is recognized as pathological by the quality of the adolescent's projections and close attention to one's countertransference, and this occurs when, rather than a love of life and knowing, there is a fundamental hatred of life and emotional knowledge, which the normally disturbed adolescent feels. Severe self-harm—such as cutting, burning, and suicide attempts—occurs in some adolescents, where the value of a new sexual body and a new inner self cannot be taken on. Body–mind confusions and splits occur at the deepest levels, so that hatred and a wish to kill can be directed at the body, in suicide and self-harm, or at the mind, in severe drug abuse and deep depressions (Bion, 1959; Laufer & Laufer, 1984; Rosenfeld, 1965, 1987).

Some borderline patients move between normal and pathological positions at different times, so that with this most disturbed group of adolescents, there may be different functions of the personality: an "adolescent function" and a "borderline function". Bion differentiated movements of the personality between neurotic and psychotic positions and, later, the operation of different functions of the personality (Bion, 1957, 1965). Each position or function needs to be separately identified and understood, then addressed, as we illustrate in the examples below. There may be movement backwards and forwards between different functions, sometimes progressively over long periods of time, sometimes erratically in a see-saw effect. There needs, too, to be a different understanding of transference in respect of each function, of normal or "neurotic" transferences and delusional or "psychotic" transferences. Clinically, it is refreshing when a patient who has been quite borderline or confused and deluded becomes disturbing in an ordinary adolescent way! There is a return to what Winnicott would term the playfulness of adolescence, driven by strong but disturbing life forces (Winnicott, 1963a, 1963b).

Freud saw the tasks of each developmental stage including adolescence as one of addressing core issues of the oedipal relationship, which means accepting the reality of new developments—of strength, power, and sexual capacity—and overcoming inhibitions and fixations to pre-oedipal relationships and fixations, including incestuous phantasies and relationships (cf. Flynn, 2000). Britton's (1989) views on the Oedipus complex can be applied here to adolescence. Just as in the depressive position some capacity to tolerate and accept loss and immediate satisfaction is necessary, so in oedipal relationships it becomes necessary to accept exclusion and restriction by not being part of the parental couple and their sexuality and hence to be able to take up what Britton calls "the third position". When internalized, this capacity to accept an actual excluded third position enables the individual to have a concept of the external, the other, in terms of his or her own experience of being an "other". This capacity to accept the other is an essential part of the adolescent taking his or her place in the world outside, in the bigger scheme of things away from the parents and the family. If the adolescent can come to accept exclusion (from the parental couple) and restriction, including the need to work towards his or her own future, then he or she gains by taking on a more secure knowledge of relations between objects, and between the parental couple, and hence gains a better knowledge of reality. If the adolescent is unable to do this or to move beyond distorted relationships with internal or external parents, he or she may harbour an "oedipal illusion" in Britton's sense.

Clinical examples

To explore more fully these theoretical ideas and their use within the treatment setting of the Adolescent Unit, as described above, we discuss three clinical examples of borderline adolescents. The three cases, Anne, Joan, and Maureen, illustrate recovery from psychotic functioning and intrapsychic growth, with concomitant improvement in social relationships and functioning.

Anne

Anne, a 17-year-old, suffered from self-harming attacks on her body and distortions in her mental states of a psychotic nature.* Her treatment showed the importance for her, and others, of an inpatient setting in which her projections could be adequately received and contained, so that she could re-establish a safer and more securely based psychic growth. Anne had been out of school since she was 10 years old, with no subsequent outside schooling. She had also been incapable of any sustained social contact or commitment outside the family, including with any groups of peers, apart from a few hours per week of home tuition. As a consequence, she suffered chronic social and personal isolation.

Anne had attended a younger-age adolescent unit for nearly two years. Subsequently she had one daily activity and her life-line—three-times-weekly private psychotherapy for two years. She was rude and contemptuous to her analyst but nevertheless made some progress.

Anne had been a bright and happy child until her parents' acrimonious divorce when she was 5 years old. She developed an omnipotent need to take responsibility, and she progressively felt her needs neglected. For two years in early adolescence, there were a number of psychotic symptoms, including a psychotic fear

---

*This case has already been described elsewhere, along with another example of a severely conduct disordered adolescent treated in the Adolescent Unit (Flynn, 2000). From the age of 14 and puberty, she was partly anorectic, severely self-harming (through disfiguring burns on her arms and legs and cuts to her face), and a substantial suicide risk.

of holding a pen, which meant she could do no schoolwork for a long period. Although these symptoms subsided, she did not change, and she remained socially isolated.

Anne continued periodically and secretly to harm herself. She was prone to idealized love phantasies of older men and was controlling in a regressed way, typified by her insistence that people—including (even especially) professionals—use a babyish form of her name. Many complied. The psychotic symptoms were not always or easily apparent; however, but real underlying change, for her to be able to take on an ordinary life, had also not occurred.

Her first month in the inpatient Adolescent Unit was an ordeal for her, which she made herself get through, sticking it out. Anne slowly began to manage the challenge of social relationships, but only as long as she kept herself emotionally distant. She and staff struggled with this, in work groups, activities, and within the twice-weekly adolescent therapy group, where her tendency to take on the role of the person responsible for keeping it all going was again particularly noticeable. In her individual psycho-therapy, what came out was her fear of putting experiences to-gether (literally "linking" and "thinking": cf. Bion, 1959, 1962a, 1962b) and having her own viewpoint, for fear of going mad. Frequently, after gaining some understanding she would evacuate it again, saying she had forgotten what happened. She could easily be forgotten by staff and some patients and remain at an emo-tional distance from others. An exception to this occurred quite atypically with one adolescent who challenged her social with-drawal as due to her personal but hidden hatred of what she located in other people. This adolescent partly bullied her, but this patient in effect also hounded her in a most useful way into a real relationship with her and to be more connected with her real needs and angry feelings!

Progressively, with her psychotherapy and her life in the unit, Anne became stronger. With a developing ego-strength, she then became more able to face more disturbing aspects of her symp-toms. For several months, she seemed to have remained on the brink of moving forward to something more normal, shown by her weight remaining just below a level where she could have regular periods until nearly the end of treatment. As she progressed, she began to attend some GCSE classes and to take more challenging roles inside and outside the hospital. In several family meetings, separately with both her father and her mother's side of the family, she began to express more about what she felt about what had happened and to understand more about her role within the family. She was temporarily less confused and isolated. Her precocious over-identification with her father, and the sexual fixations on older men, were still, however, more apparent to us than to her, as was her mother's depression and incapacity to bear feelings. It was now apparent that there had been at crucial times, particularly after the divorce, a chronic pattern of almost complete denial of emotionality within the family.

A significant point of progress in her treatment came when Anne allowed herself to re-experience towards the end of treatment a reactivation of her suicide wishes. A particularly stressful and terrifying incident occurred at home on one of the final weekends in the run-up to discharge. Anne tried to jump out of a second-floor window and had to be restrained by her stepfather. What happened could then, after many months of treatment and family work, be recognized by Anne and her parents and subsequently be thought about and discussed within Anne's treatment. Anne could now see that this alarming behaviour could represent something. Anne now had an increased capacity to allow her real feelings to be expressed, however disturbed. This allowed her to work to differentiate more her powerful but largely hidden emotions and to use projective identification, less in a negative way— by breaking links of understanding, leading to psychotic manifestations, and acts of self-harm—but more as means of communication (cf. Bion, 1962a, 1962b). In this instance, in a trip out with her family to a cafe that afternoon, she had experienced an outburst of pathological jealousy about another girl they had met whom she felt that others, particularly her mother, were more interested in than her. This could be linked to her pathological jealousy of her younger sister and be seen as part of a pattern of her intense emotions, and other conflicts about her mother and father, on an infantile level and as a child after the divorce, rather than as something that was simply mad.

In one meeting of the adolescents near the end of treatment, she talked with some clarity about her feelings and wishes and withstood some of the conflict and hostility coming at her from other adolescents within the meeting. I noticed her fiddling about continuously with a pen with her proper name on it, "Anne", which she normally would never use or want others to use. She knew I always called her "Anne", much to her annoyance, and never the babyish form of her name that she usually insisted on. Something important was symbolized in this small act. With her increased capacity for social relationships, and her increased ego-strength, I thought she was beginning to build a new clearer identity, less regressed and hostile, but with a sense, too, of where she stood socially. The pen that had once been feared in a psychotic way she now could hold. It was just a pen, and she fiddled about with it nervously, as she struggled within the group meeting. Previously her fear of the pen had created enormous disabilities for her, taking away her education and social life. Now, since she had more capacity to contain her emotions and experiences, the pen was more like, in Winnicott's terms, a transitional object (Winnicott, 1971c). Anne was learning that she could leave behind her some of her infantile identifications and could begin to manage within a group of adolescents and be able to contain herself.

Joan

Joan, aged 16 years, used a number of aspects of therapeutic-community treatment to overcome a severe depression. In particular, we illustrate how she experienced in the here-and-now of the treatment, especially in its later phases, a depth of feelings which enabled her to complete the year-long inpatient experience in an emotionally real way. She had taken six overdoses since the age of 14, the last of which nearly killed her, putting her in a coma for some days. She was on a Section 3 until the week before admission because she had said that after her GCSEs she planned to kill herself.*

---

*A Section 3 is a compulsory treatment section of the Mental Health Act 1987, valid for six months, which allows the patient to be detained and treated without his or her consent.

It was quite unusual to transfer after just a weekend's break from an acute adolescent unit to the Cassel Hospital. We would normally require a minimum interval of two weeks between transfer at home, or in a non-hospital setting. We did so in this case because of the anxiety about her.

Joan's parents had divorced when she was a year old, and she had lived first with her mother then her father after an extended and relentless custody battle. Joan's mother suffers from a chronic and severe manic-depressive psychosis, with schizophrenic tendencies, and Joan was left with her alone for many of the early months of her life. Joan, when subsequently with her father, had actually been mothered by her grandmother until she was 6 years old, when her father remarried and the grandmother went back to Scotland. She later died without Joan ever seeing her again. The anger she felt about this was displaced onto the stepmother. The situation was exacerbated further when the stepmother "persuaded" her to ask her mother to stop all contact with her when she was aged 10, because contact had been bizarre and upsetting for Joan. In her upbringing, Joan had clearly been disturbed by her mother and unable to express and work through her sense of responsibility for her mother and her confused and intense sense of guilt. She had attempted to cut off and kill off her unwanted thoughts, which left her feeling more desperate and alone, and then she tried the overdoses, to kill herself off.

This pattern of cutting off from others repeated itself in the early part of treatment. The Cassel Adolescent Unit is more open and free than the heavily structured unit she had been in, where she had "buried" herself in her GCSE work. Gradually she became more involved. Renewed attachments were formed within her family, with her father and stepmother, especially with the support of family meetings. She made new relationships in the therapeutic community, and importantly she worked through broken relationships with changes of first nurses. Joan was amazed that people were genuinely interested in how she was and what she felt, especially in her individual psychotherapy. From these experiences, she began to understand more about the central underlying problem of separation. She experienced separations as that person dying and, due to her complex unconscious guilt, that she had killed off the person. She felt this in relation to her mother and her grandmother. She was also frightened of her natural mother pushing things into her. It seemed evident that at a very early age there had been, and continued to be, as a matter of reality, some level of psychotic impingement from the mother. In her transference to her psychotherapist and in her relation to nurses, Joan had to work to discriminate what was "mad" from what she could accept. This problem of "taking in" may have been related to the eating problem she had and to her resistance to hearing what people were saying to her about what she would need. To avoid this painful "taking in", if she could set aside the loving feelings she had had for her grandmother, she could also set aside the feeling that she had killed her. However, the result of this was that she became even more cut off from her needs.

Despite work on this, Joan still managed to keep a degree of her real affect and some aspects of her whole development out of treatment. A relationship, partly sexual, to another young woman who had left the hospital kept the transference within the hospital a bit diluted, as well as keeping to the side issues of her personal and sexual identity. Joan wanted instead to get back to school to do A levels, and to be coated again with a secure sense of normality. She complained about how "mad" we all were to expect her to engage in treatment any more. Her dispute with us over her leaving date—she wanted to leave earlier by about a month—brought all this to a head. We challenged her, and this brought out an open disagreement on the issue for about two months. Her full anger and fury were now expressed, about endings and the separation from the hospital, in a way that clearly helped her see her real level of feelings in many other areas too. This intense resurgence of her affect around the issue of separation from treatment, and its containment, helped in effect to re-engage Joan in treatment in a crucial way and at a crucial time. The immediate problems of her conflict with us in the therapeutic-community setting recreated problems from the past and core intrapsychic issues for her, which connected to the fundamental dynamic of her suicidal feelings and her anger with all her close parental figures. Eventually a compromise was reached that worked well, whereby she started classes outside the hospital but came back for about two further weeks of psychotherapy and her final review.

Maureen

Maureen, referred to earlier, is our final example. We describe the occurrence and understanding of delusional symptoms as part of a pattern of disturbance of an abused young woman with a severe borderline personality disorder. We aim to show that those who suffer from borderline personality disorders may move between more normal/neurotic positions and more psychotic positions (Bion, 1957, 1965; Rosenfeld, 1965, 1987). In other words, at times of severe disturbance, normal and neurotic levels of functioning break down, and such patients show a psychotic level of disturbance. This needs to be understood, in order to work to re-establish a more normal and neurotic level of functioning.

Maureen is a young woman of 20 years who came to the Cassel following a very disturbed upbringing. She was one of two children in a family in which the parents were together but both had had considerable mental health difficulties. The mother made repeated self-harm and suicide attempts, frequently in front of her daughter, who then had to call for help. The father had suffered major depression and was felt by Maureen to be cruel, undermining, and useless, in that he did nothing for the family. Maureen had suffered sexual abuse from a family friend over a prolonged period between the ages of 9 and 13 years. She was involved between her parents in their recurring violent conflicts, and she became incapable of secure, long-lasting external attachments outside the family. The severe conflicts were now internalized. She had had repeated disturbances, including self-harm and suicide attempts, since the age of 14 years. The dependence of her parents on psychiatric services now translated into Maureen's parasitic dependence on psychiatric services, especially recurrent and ineffective inpatient psychiatric admissions. Bion described how such parasitic relationships destroy both sides (Bion, 1970, p. 103).

On admission Maureen complained of not knowing who she was. She was seen to have a confused identity, significant obsessional rituals, and extensive concrete thinking. Examples of this come out below. She was very overweight, although she had had a period of being very slim when infatuated with a female teacher. Prior to admission to the Cassel, she used alcohol excessively. Two types of self-harm were most prominent. There had been multiple severe depth slashes by a knife or razor on both arms. To someone seeing these first off, they have a gruesome effect and could make one feel sick. There was also the ever-looming possibility that a serious suicide attempt would be made, in a final way that would end everything. Behind this was her recurring fear of going mad.

What also became prominent within the treatment were major worrying incidents where threats were made on the lives of staff working with her. Due to states of confusion, her aggression against people outside would often be seen by her to be legitimized. Following a first aggressive incident, Maureen was away from the hospital for three to four weeks, some of the time back in her local psychiatric hospital. Later on, there was another absence from the hospital, when she was on short leave for nearly two weeks. There were then severe anxieties about her capacity to sustain our sort of treatment. We shall return to this period of absence and short leave below to look at the meaning of her self-harm.

Maureen was one of the most worrying adolescents on the unit at that time. Her obsessional rituals manifested themselves across the hospital, particularly in the activities and work-groups, preventing her being really involved. It was always difficult to get at what exactly Maureen's emotional state was, as there was extensive splitting of her experience. Simultaneous traits existed, of mocking withdrawal and manic excited exuberance, and she evoked complicity by seduction with some staff and anger and rejection in other staff. It was difficult to get through to Maureen, and there was a doubt about whether she could take anything in. The significance of this may date from her earliest infantile experience, for we knew that as an infant Maureen suffered from seizures and was also hospitalized because of being unable to digest milk.

Within treatment, Maureen had now settled into a pattern in which she used alcohol outside the hospital each weekend, thereby blotting out her capacity to react to and further her involvement, and preventing real advances in treatment. The first serious violent incident occurred when, rejecting the night nurse's involvement with her, she brandished a knife at her, again under the influence of alcohol. We understood the violence to have erupted because she was being challenged. Her obsessional rituals had served to keep out troubling and conflicting emotions, but at a deeper level they served, too, to keep out a psychotic level of confusion. When her behaviour was challenged, she began to act in a bizarre and dangerous way. We decided only to allow her to return to the hospital after she had agreed a contract not to use alcohol within her treatment. This was stricter and less flexible than rules about alcohol with other patients. However, such stricter boundaries allowed for more productive periods of treatment, when she could listen and so be less paranoid and less constantly misunderstanding of the motives of others. She could then develop some relationships in the community, where she became in time increasingly well-liked and, for some patients, almost indispensable for their treatment. This reflected within the therapeutic culture how Maureen could be again, as in her family, the indispensable helper who could set herself apart from personal conflicts. This was a kind of "oedipal illusion" in Ron Britton's sense (1989), where she could be the only helpful one and there was seen to be no helpful parental couple or parental authority.

We shall describe now the build-up over a two- to three-week period, setting the scene to the second period away from the hospital and our understanding then of her behaviour and her disturbance. Maureen had the staff split in her mind. There were just one or two figures that were helpful, and most figures were mistrusted. She had an obsessional, paranoid belief that the head of the Adolescent Unit was out to kill her, and there were other disturbing examples of concrete thinking. Helpful and genuine interventions were treated either with disdain or as directly provocative and troubling. Evident in her, at a deeper level, was a destructive envy and a fateful hopelessness.

Maureen kept stressing at this time how crazy her mother was and how her mother kept upsetting her, particularly at weekends. Nevertheless, when in her flat at weekends, she had to be in contact with her parents three times a day, otherwise she would not manage. She was upset also about a worker, from the voluntary society that had helped her, who had recently left. All the signs were there of a recurring pattern for her of an idealized relationship, or infatuation, with some degree of over-involve-ment by the worker with her. This could be understood as a splitting of the bad intrusive mother (her real mother) and the replacement idealized mother (the worker and, sometimes during treatment, her psychotherapist). Maureen had always had a pride in her own flat which she kept comfortable and pristine. Every effort and most resources were put into keeping the flat so. By contrast, it was very difficult to get her to put the same level of emotional resources into her treatment. A worrying warning sign occurred one weekend when she smashed a number of treasured ornaments in her flat in a fit of rage.

Also over this time, Maureen became increasingly and continu-ally preoccupied that something would get into her flat to spoil it and ruin it from the inside. This seemed to fit with a level of paranoid thinking, in every aspect of contact with her, that some-thing evil or bad would destroy her from the inside. Contamina-tion could get into everything and could get anywhere. Suddenly this fear became a reality for her, when she discovered some maggots in her flat. Evidently a neighbour, a fisherman, had been breeding maggots in his flat, and somehow or other some of these had got into her flat. It was difficult to know how real the problem was. There was something confused and unreal about the whole thing, but while she was preoccupied with this, there was no way that anything at the Cassel could be thought about. All attention had to be paid to the infestation within the flat. Maureen was now becoming more worrying within the hospital. Some of what she said seemed confused and had a psychotic feel about it, although there was no evidence that she was hallucinating in a formally psychotic way.

During this time Maureen had her first family meeting with her mother and father, together with her nurse and the head of the unit. To the workers, and indeed the family at the time, there was a sense that some understanding of various matters had been shared. It was noticeable, however, how Maureen's mother did continually interrupt or talk over her, indeed invade her, as she remained obliviously and continually preoccupied about herself. In turn, Maureen obliterated anything helpful her father said, and he was not capable of pulling anything together. Maureen mentioned, but her parents passed over, the incidents in childhood with the family friend, and it seemed that the issue of sexual abuse could not be talked about.

Following the family meeting, nevertheless, Maureen seemed temporarily for a day or two less disturbed. However, her mind was bent on going off for a week on short leave to sort out her flat with the environmental health officer, and various other issues about benefits, which did need dealing with. She was prevailed upon to reduce this period to two days and therefore was going to return on the Tuesday night instead of the Sunday night from the weekend at home. There was some breakdown in the communication between staff about the arrangements—a sign that could later be seen as evidence of a splitting process.

On the Monday night, the first day of short leave, a very serious incident occurred when Maureen severely cut herself at her flat, in a similar manner to previous severe acts of self-harm. She was admitted to her local psychiatric hospital, reportedly with some depersonalization and a risk of suicide.

On the psychiatric ward, her behaviour returned to normal within a few days. After some ten days and several meetings with the psychiatrist there and the workers here, she returned to the Cassel and settled back into treatment. Similar patterns subsequently occurred. Maureen's treatment continued, and there were periods of progress and periods of acute disturbance and, in an overall sense, some improvement.

For our purposes now, we shall attempt to use our understanding of what happened and what led to this episode of self-harm. We shall describe the transition to an increased level of psychotic functioning, followed by more cooperation in treatment and progress, with the re-establishment of a normal or neurotic level of functioning.

The meaning of Maureen's self-harm on this occasion can be understood, but only in a very complex way, and only by putting together many aspects of the treatment. In particular we need to examine her relation to the tasks and activities in the hospital, her relationships with the nurses, and what she was able to work through in an individual transference within her therapy. It would seem that Maureen had been deeply affected by continuous worrying and meaningless intrusions, particularly from her mother. Her own thinking and mind was continually invaded. This repeated the effect of her mother's suicidal and self-harming attacks during her childhood, which had also brought with it a real level of emotional deprivation. Maureen had then suffered a further type of intrusion, in terms of the sexual abuse by the family friend. It is unclear whether there was parental complicity in this, but at least it is clear that there was some negligence.

Maureen's own mental functioning developed in a way that had made her mistrustful, paranoid, and prone to severe splitting, coupled with patterns of destructive fragmentation leading to confusional states. This type of functioning is well described by Herbert Rosenfeld (1965), Wilfred Bion (1957), and Melanie Klein (1946). Central to this is the severe splitting of mind and body. Freud spoke of the ego as "a bodily ego". Maureen, with her severe level of splitting, could enact a destructive threat on herself by attacking her body, hence the severe cutting. When this splitting occurred, there were the good and bad workers; there was also the good place and the bad place, the good place being the idealized flat, the bad place being the troubling and disquieting Cassel Hospital. Anna Freud, in a Yale Law School seminar (quoted in Schechter, 1967), has described how, at a neurotic level of functioning, severely deprived children often enact a split within themselves in which the body is neglected and mistreated but then needs to be looked after by someone. Effectively, then, the child internalizes a helper and a helped. Maureen's concentration in an obsessional way on cleaning her flat—and, indeed, her self-appointed role of helper of other patients on the unit—was this helping activity in relation to the damaged part of the self. So long as Maureen could keep up this idealized form of care, at a relatively static level of severe neurotic conflict, regarding herself as able to maintain her flat and her place within the unit, there was less likelihood of a psychotic level of reaction. Below her level of ordinary or neurotic difficulties, then, and the obsessional symptoms, was potentially a psychotic level of mental activity and disturbance. It was when her neurotic level of adaptation eventually entirely broke down on the Monday, and her flat went from being very good, or ideal, to very bad and contaminated, that

Maureen reverted to a psychotic level of functioning and, with renewed severe splitting, made the severe attacks on her body. This led in turn to a severe sense of hopelessness and a more worrying danger that a real suicide attempt would be made.

These delusional ideas took over Maureen when she was pushing away and withdrawing from contact and treatment. Her thinking had become more concrete (Segal, 1957), she was attacking the unit and its head, but then the projective identification was returned in a concrete form in her paranoid idea that he "was out to kill her", and she needed to get out of the hospital (Bion, 1954, 1956). Her ideas became progressively more paranoid and her previous idealizations, about her previous worker and her flat, broke down, leading her to experience fully the terrifying splitting and fragmentation within herself, leading then to attacks on herself, the severe self-harm, and the danger of a suicide attempt.

Our subsequent work with this patient has tried to incorporate what we had learnt about the build-up to this self-harm. We felt it necessary to work, particularly in the individual therapy, with the way sometimes rather incomplete and indeed thin levels of contact became idealized. Maureen would then become obsessed with the idea that she was going to lose what little she had. All the while, however, contact within the therapeutic community—which was indeed potentially more helpful, richer, and could have a more purposeful direction—would get over-looked. There was a calmer aspect to Maureen as she took on some of this. She then began to use more normal therapeutic structures as a vehicle for expression of her conflicts, as illustrated above in an earlier example about her use of the work-group to express feelings in her relationship with her nurse.

Conclusion

In these case descriptions of Anne, Joan, and Maureen, we can see adolescents who were able to use aspects of the therapeutic community and psychoanalytic psychotherapy. They were able to recover from states of acute disturbance, characterized by delusional states and psychotic symptoms, so creating again a push for ordinary adolescent expression, change, and development. Bion (1962) introduced the concept of "containment", using the example of the child's earliest object relations in relation to the breast, to describe the modification of infantile fears. The infant projects a part of its psyche—namely, its bad feelings—into a good breast, then, in due course, they are removed and re-introjected. During their sojourn in the good breast, they are felt to have been modified in such a way that the object that is re-introjected has become tolerable to the infant's psyche. The "container" is that into which an object is projected, and the "contained" is that which can be projected into the "container" (Bion, 1962a, p. 90). Adapting this theory of containment to the study of adolescents, the "contained" in the Adolescent Unit may at times be certain bizarre and psychotic manifestations from the adolescent, and at other times more lively yet still disturbed expressions of adolescent change and development. The "container" is both the receptive emotional capacities of the staff, nurses, and psychotherapists and their thoughtful structures for realistic communal living, in the therapeutic culture of the unit and the hospital, as devised through the cooperative capacities of therapeutic community residents. We have described in the examples how work derived from psychoanalytic thinking and the patients' engagement in socially productive roles may help them move away from illness and develop new active ego strengths to create real internal and external change.

REFERENCES

Ainsworth, M. D. S., Blehar, M. C., Waters, E., & Wall, S. (1978). *Patterns of Attachment: A Psychological Study of the Strange Situation.* Hillsdale, NJ: Erlbaum.

Anderson, R., & Dartington, A. (1998). *Facing It Out: Clinical Perspectives on Adolescent Disturbance.* London: Duckworth.

Aries, P. (1985). *Centuries of Childhood.* Harmondsworth: Peregrine.

Arnold, M. (1867). Dover Beach. In: *New Poems.* London: Macmillan and Co.

Audit Commission (1999). *Children in Mind: Child and Adolescent Mental Health Services.* London: HMSO.

Bandler, D. (1987). Working with other professionals in an inpatient setting. *Journal of Child Psychotherapy, 13* (2).

Barnes, E. (Ed.) (1968). *Psychosocial nursing.* London: Tavistock.

Barnes, E., Griffiths, P., Ord, J., & Wells, D. (Eds.) (1997). *Face to Face with Distress: The Professional Use of Self in Psychosocial Care.* Oxford: Butterworth Heinemann.

Barrett, M., & Trevitt, J. (1991). *Attachment Behaviour and the Schoolchild: An Introduction to Educational Therapy.* London: Routledge.

Bennathan, M., & Boxall, M. (1996). *Effective Intervention in Primary Schools: Nurture Groups.* London: David Fulton.

Bick, E. (1968). The experience of skin in early object relationships. *International Journal of Psycho-Analysis, 49:* 484–486.

Bion, W. R. (1954). Notes on the theory of schizophrenia. In: *Second Thoughts*. London: Heinemann, 1967.

Bion, W. R. (1956). Development of schizophrenic thought. In: *Second Thoughts*. London: Heinemann, 1967.

Bion, W. R. (1957). Differentiation of the psychotic from the non-psychotic personalities. In: *Second Thoughts*. London: Heinemann, 1967.

Bion, W. R. (1958). On hallucination. In: *Second Thoughts*. London: Heinemann, 1967.

Bion, W. R. (1959). Attacks on linking. In: *Second Thoughts*. London: Heinemann, 1967.

Bion, W. R. (1961). *Experiences in Groups*. London: Routledge.

Bion, W. R. (1962a). *Learning from Experience*. London: Heinemann.

Bion, W. R. (1962b). A theory of thinking. *International Journal of Psycho-Analysis*, 43: 306–310. Also in: *Second Thoughts*. London: Heinemann, 1967.

Bion, W. R. (1963). *Elements of Psychoanalysis*. London: Tavistock.

Bion, W. R. (1965). *Transformations*. London: Tavistock. Also in: *Seven Servants*. New York: Jason Aronson, 1977.

Bion, W. R. (1970). *Attention and Interpretation*. London: Tavistock.

Black, D., et al. (1993). *When Father Kills Mother: Guiding Children through Trauma and Grief*. London: Routledge.

Blos, P. (1979). *The Adolescent Passage: Developmental Issues*. Madison, CT: International Universities Press.

Bowlby, J. (1969). *Attachment and Loss, Vol. 1*. London: Penguin.

Bowlby, J. (1988). *A Secure Base: Clinical Applications of Attachment Theory*. London: Routledge.

Britton, R. (1989). The missing link: parental sexuality in the Oedipus complex. In: R. Britton, M. Feldman, & E. O'Shaughnessy (Eds.), *The Oedipus Complex Today*. London: Karnac.

Copeley, B. (1993). *The World of Adolescence: Literature, Society and Psychoanalytic Psychotherapy*. London: Free Association Books.

Dingwall, R., Eeklaar, J., & Murray, T. (1983). *The Protection of Children: State Intervention and Family Life*. Oxford: Blackwell.

Dwivedi, K. N., & Varma, V. P. (1997). *Depression in Children and Adolescents*. London: Whurr.

Flynn, C. (1993). The patient's pantry: the nature of the nursing task. *Therapeutic Communities*, 14 (4).

Flynn, D. (1987). The child's view of the hospital: an examination of the child's experience of an inpatient setting. In: R. Kennedy, A. Heymans, & L. Tischler (Eds.), *The Family In-patient*. London: Free Association Books.

Flynn, D. (1988). The assessment and psychotherapy of a physically abused girl during in-patient family treatment. *Journal of Child Psychotherapy, 13* (2).

Flynn, D. (1999). The challenges of in-patient work in a therapeutic community. In: M. Lanyado & A. Horne (Eds.), *The Handbook of Child and Adolescent Psychotherapy*. London: Routledge.

Flynn, D. (2000). Adolescence. In: I. Wise (Ed.), *Adolescence*. Psychoanalytic Ideas Series. London: Institute of Psychoanalysis.

Foster, A. (1998). Psychotic processes and community care: the difficulty in finding the third position. In: A. Foster & V. Zagier Roberts (Eds.), *Managing Mental Health in the Community: Chaos and Containment*. London: Routledge.

Freud, A. (1936). *The Ego and Mechanisms of Defence*. London: Hogarth Press.

Freud, S. (1895b [1894]). On the grounds for detaching a particular syndrome from neurasthenia under the description "anxiety neurosis", *S.E., Vol. 3* (pp. 87–120).

Freud, S. (1895d) (with Breuer, J.). *Studies on Hysteria. S.E., Vol. 2.*

Freud, S. (1914c). On narcissism: an introduction. *S.E., Vol. 14* (pp. 67–104).

Freud, S. (1916a). On transience. *S.E., Vol. 14* (pp. 303–308).

Geddes, H. (1999). Attachment behaviour and learning: implications for the pupil, the teacher and the task. *Educational Therapy and Therapeutic Teaching, 8:* 20–34.

Green, M. (1996). Using fairy tales with children. *Educational Therapy and Therapeutic Teaching, 5:* 18–35.

Greenhalgh, P. (1994). *Emotional Growth and Learning*. London: Routledge.

Griffiths, P., & Leach, G. (1997). Psychosocial nursing: a model learnt from experience. In: E. Barnes, P. Griffiths, J. Ord, & D. Wells (Eds), *Face to Face with Distress: The Professional Use of Self in Psychosocial Care*. London: Butterworth Heinemann.

Griffiths, P., & Pringle, P. (Eds.) (1997). *Psychosocial Practice within a Residential setting*. London: Karnac.

HAS (1986). *Bridges over Troubled Waters*. NHS Health Advisory Service. London: HMSO.

Heimann, P. (1950). On counter-transference. *International Journal of Psycho-Analysis, 31:* 81–84.

High, H. (1985). The use of indirect communication in educational therapy. *Journal of Educational Therapy, 1* (3): 3–18.

Holditch, L. (1995). Learning: only a game? *Educational Therapy and Therapeutic Teaching, 4:* 34–43.

Holmes, E. (2000). Nurture groups—a therapeutic intervention. *Educational Therapy and Therapeutic Teaching, 9:* 58–65.

Hopkins, J. (1986). Solving the mystery of monsters: steps towards the recovery from trauma. *Journal of Child Psychotherapy, 12* (1).

James, O. (1986). The role of the nurse/therapist relationship in the therapeutic community. In: R. Kennedy, A. Heymans, & L. Tischler (Eds.), *The Family as In-patient.* London: Free Association Books.

Kennedy, R. (1986). Work of the day: aspects of work with families at the Cassel Hospital. In: R. Kennedy, A Heymans, & L. Tischler (Eds.), *The Family as In-patient.* London: Free Association Books.

Kennedy, R. (1989). Psychotherapy, child abuse and the law. *Bulletin of the Royal College of Psychiatrists, 13:* 471–476.

Kennedy, R. (1997). *Child Abuse, Psychotherapy and the Law.* London: Free Association Books.

Kennedy, R., & Coombe, P. (1995). Family treatment of Munchhausen syndrome by proxy. *Bulletin of the Australian Association of Group Psychotherapists, 15:* 1–8.

Kennedy, R., Heymans, A., & Tischler, L. (Eds.) (1986). *The Family as In-patient.* London: Free Association Books.

Klein, M. (1932). The technique of analysis in puberty. In: *The Psycho-Analysis of Children. Writings, Vol. 2.* London: Hogarth Press, 1975.

Klein, M. (1946). Notes on some schizoid mechanisms. In: *Envy, Gratitude and Other Works, 1946–1963. Writings, Vol. 3.* London: Hogarth Press, 1975.

Klein, M. (1957). Envy and gratitude. In: *Envy and Gratitude and Other Works 1946–1963. Writings, Vol. 3.* London: Hogarth Press, 1975.

Kroger, J. C. (1996). *Identity in Adolescence: The Balance between Self and Other,* 2nd edition. London: Routledge.

Laufer, M., & Laufer, E. (1984). *Adolescence and Developmental Breakdown: A Psychoanalytic View.* London: Karnac, 1995.

Loader, P., & Kelly, C. (1996). Munchhausen syndrome by proxy: a narrative approach to explanation. *Clinical Child Psychology and Psychiatry, 1* (3): 353–363.

Main, T. (1957). The ailment. In: *The Ailment and Other Psychoanalytic Essays,* ed J. Johns. London: Free Association Books, 1989.

Meadow, R. (1977). Munchhausen's syndrome by proxy: the hinterland of child abuse. *The Lancet, 2:* 343–345.

Meltzer, H., & Gatward, R. (2000). *The Mental Health of Children and Adolescents in Great Britain: Summary Report of Office for National Statistics.* London: HMSO.

Menzies Lyth, I. (1979). Staff support systems: task and anti-task in adolescent institutions. In: *Containing Anxiety in Institutions*. London: Free Association Books, 1988.

Morton, G. (1996). The therapeutic potential of story making with children. *Educational Therapy and Therapeutic Teaching, 5*: 5–17.

Morton, G. (2000a). Educational therapy: challenges and possibilities of work in different settings. *Educational Therapy and Therapeutic Teaching, 9*: 39–57.

Morton, G. (2000b). Working with stories in groups. In: N. Barwick (Ed.), *Clinical Counselling in Schools* (pp. 142–158). London: Routledge.

Muir, B. (1986). Is in-patient psychotherapy a valid concept? In: R. Kennedy, A. Heymans, & L. Tischler (Eds.), *The Family as Inpatient*. London: Free Association Books.

Obholzer, A., & Roberts, V. Z. (Eds.) (1994). *The Unconscious at Work*. London: Routledge.

Parton, N. (1991). *Governing the Family: Child Care, Child Protection and the State*. London: Macmillan.

Racker, H. (1968). *Transference and Countertransference*. London: Karnac, 1988.

Rosenfeld, H. A. (1965). *Psychotic States*. London: Karnac, 1990.

Rosenfeld, H. A. (1987). *Impasse and Interpretation*. London: Tavistock.

Rutter, M., & Rutter, M. (1993). *Developing Minds: Challenge and Continuity across the Lifespan*. London: Penguin.

Salzberger-Wittenberg, I., Henry, G., & Osborne, E. (1983). *The Emotional Experience of Learning and Teaching*. London: Routledge & Kegan Paul.

Schechter, M. D. (1967). Psychoanalytic theory as it relates to adoption. *Journal of the American Psycho-Analytical Association, 15*, 695–708.

Schreier, H. A. (1992). The perversion of mothering: Munchhausen syndrome by proxy. *Bulletin of the Menninger Clinic, 56*: 421–437.

Segal, H. (1957). Notes on symbol formation. In: *The Work of Hannah Segal: Delusion and Artistic Creativity and Other Psychoanalytic Essays*. London: Free Association Books.

Shaffer, D., & Piancentini, J. (1994). Suicide and attempted suicide. In: M. Rutter, E. Taylor, & L. Hersor (Eds.), *Child and Adolescent Psychiatry: Modern Approaches*. Oxford: Blackwell Scientific.

Stern, D. (1985). *The Interpersonal World of the Infant*. New York: Basic Books.

Stokes, J. (1994). The unconscious at work in groups and teams: contribution from the work of Wilfred Bion. In: V. Zagier Roberts & A. Obholzer (Eds.), *The Unconscious at Work*. London: Routledge.

Target, M., & Fonagy, P. (1996). The psychological treatment of child and adolescent psychiatric disorders. In: A. Roth & P. Fonagy, *What Works for Whom? A Critical Review of Psychotherapy Research*. London: Guildford Press.

Tischler, L. (1986). Nurse/therapist supervision. In: R. Kennedy, A. Heymans, & L. Tischler (Eds.), *The Family as In-patient*. London: Free Association Books.

Waddell, M. (1998). *Inside Lives*. London: Duckworth.

Welldon, E. (1992). *Mother, Madonna, Whore*. London: Guilford Press.

Williams, M. (1992). *The Velveteen Rabbit*. London: Mammoth.

Winnicott, D. W. (1951). Transitional objects and transitional phenomena. In: *Through Paediatrics to Psycho-Analysis*. London: Hogarth Press, 1975.

Winnicott, D. W. (1961). Adolescence: struggling through the doldrums. In: *Through Paediatrics to Psycho-Analysis*. London: Hogarth Press, 1975.

Winnicott, D. W. (1963a). Communicating and not communicating leading to a study of certain opposites. In: *The Maturational Processes and the Facilitating Environment*. London: Hogarth Press, 1965.

Winnicott, D. W. (1963b). Hospital care supplementing intensive psychotherapy in adolescence. In: *The Maturational Processes and the Facilitating Environment*. London: Hogarth Press, 1965.

Winnicott, D. W. (1964). *The Child, the Family and the Outside World*. London: Penguin.

Winnicott, D. W. (1966). The ordinary devoted mother. In: *Babies and Their Mothers*. London: Free Association Books, 1987.

Winnicott, D. W. (1968a). Contemporary concepts of adolescent development and their implications for higher education. In: *Playing and Reality*. London: Tavistock Publications, 1971.

Winnicott, D. W. (1968b). Communication between infant and mother, and mother and infant, compared and contrasted. In: *Babies and Their Mothers*. London: Free Association Books, 1987.

Winnicott, D. W. (1971a). Mirror role of mother and father in child development. In: *Playing and Reality*. London: Tavistock Publications.

Winnicott, D. W. (1971b). Playing: the search for the self. In: *Playing and Reality*, Penguin Books.

Winnicott, D. W. (1971c). *Playing and Reality*. London: Tavistock Publications.

Zetzel, E. (1970). *The Capacity For Emotional Growth*. London: Hogarth.

INDEX

abandonment, fear of, 21
abuse:
  child(hood), 6–9, 11, 15, 25, 32, 36,
      37, 67
    sexual, 20, 21, 24, 26, 30, 33, 152,
      166, 170, 171
    see also clinical examples: Loretta;
      Ms Smith and Jane
abusive family, 1
adolescence:
  concept of, 2
  playfulness of [Winnicott], 159
  psychodynamic theories of, 2
  as time of transitions, 107–126, 156
  work of, 113
adolescent(s):
  borderline, containment and
      treatment of, 127–145, 147–173
  diagnosable disorder of,
      epidemiological studies of, 2
  doldrums [Winnicott], 110
  function, 12
    vs. borderline function, 156–159
  mental health services for,
      establishment of, 2
  and therapeutic community,

reciprocal impact of, 11
Adolescent Service, Cassel Hospital:
    see Cassel Hospital,
      Adolescent Service
Adolescent Unit, Cassel Hospital, 38,
      60, 115, 116, 121, 132, 147
  containment provided in, 11, 128–
      145, 149
    for staff, 121, 144
  life on, 116
  treatment structures in, 149
  see also clinical examples: Anne;
      Caroline; Joan; John, Judy;
      Mary; Maureen; Rachel
adult psychotherapy, 8
aggression, 7, 59, 134, 167
Ainsworth, M. D. S., 87, 92
analysability, criteria of, 58
Anderson, R., 2, 4, 108, 125
anger, of abused child [clinical
      example: Loretta], 35–56
anxiety:
  neurosis, 109
  separation, 21, 25, 35, 42, 66, 71, 80,
      128, 137
Aries, P., 2